ON THE OTHER SIDE OF THE FENCE

RISK, REWARD, AND OPENING DOORS

Luis G. Martinez

Cover photo credit- Chris Buchanan

Foreword

For most people, getting fuel for their car is a very simple process. You pull up to the pump, enter your credit card, fill the tank and drive away when done. But where does that fuel come from? And how is gasoline made?

I'm lucky to have worked with Graham Martinez for over six years and benefit from his high level of focus and performance. But I've also been lucky to learn more about the man and his laser focus on developing a team. How did this come about?

In Graham's book, he gives us a glimpse into the very complex and dangerous world of refining crude oil in various projects we use in our daily lives. But there's more to his story as we learn the making of a man. From a very rough start, without a lot of breaks, how did this one man grow into a very successful individual and especially a very successful mentor and leader? That's the true story of "On the Other Side of the Fence".

Tom McCartin

Senior Director of Fuel Management at Spirit Airlines

ON THE OTHER SIDE OF THE FENCE

RISK, REWARD, AND OPENING DOORS

BY

Luis Graham Martinez

*"I've seen fire and I've seen rain
I've seen sunny days that I thought would never end"*

James Taylor

This book is dedicated to:

My family.

The people of the Yorktown Refinery, who taught me everything I know. The fires are out, and the machines are all quiet. We served our country and community by providing fuels that powered America for almost 60 years.

To my teams in Paulsboro and Orlando.

May our memories and stories live on forever.

TABLE OF CONTENTS

Foreword iii

Introduction 1

PART I: Building an Outstanding Leader 3

    Chapter One: Can Anyone Hear Me? 5

    Chapter Two: Bankruptcy, Divorce, and the Roaches 13

PART II: The Refined Life 21

    Chapter Three: The Refinery Smells Like Money 23

    Chapter Four: This Place Was Lit 36

    Chapter Five: The Big Shutdown 49

Part III: It's a Terminal Now 53

    Chapter Six: Same Address, Different Place 54

    Chapter Seven: Paulsboro, New Jersey 61

    Chapter Eight: A Different Siege of Yorktown 68

    Chapter Nine: A Camper, an Airport, and a Dream 73

Part IV: Leadership Mentality 87

    Chapter Ten: Old Fashioned Hard Work ... 90

    Chapter Eleven: We Won't Quit 104

Epilogue/Conclusion 108

Bibliography 111
Acknowledgments 113
About the Author 116

Introduction

Have you ever driven by a big industrial complex, chemical plant, oil terminal, or refinery, and wondered, what goes on there or how does that work? A refinery is a city within a city, it has its own culture and cliques, danger, and peril around every corner.

This book chronicles what life is like inside of the gates, the ups and downs, the good days and the bad. Fires, explosions, burns, spills, these things happen. As you will read, sometimes far too often. First-hand accounts, based on my experience as an emergency responder, and others that I worked with. You will learn how crude oil from all over the globe ends up in your fuel tank. If you ever wondered what makes one gas station fuel different from another, read on.

This is also a personal story about opportunity and making the most of it. From growing up in a lower to middle income family, adoption, premature birth, bankruptcy, to managing the fuel operation at one of the world's busiest airports. My journey in petroleum unlocked a world of opportunity, all from hard work, good luck, and great timing.

What I hope you will learn are some good life lessons, how the petroleum industry works, and maybe a thing or two about leadership. How preparation and hard work can put you in the best position to succeed. Picking up and moving forward after a disaster applies to my personal and professional life. All of that is described in my journey, which has been as complex as the refinery I worked in. Thank you for coming along, I have quite a story to tell.

My story is about-

- Overcoming adversity

- Petroleum refineries, dangers, and opportunities

- How these things made me an award-winning leader

These three things come together in this book. The adversity that I faced in my early life, combined with the lessons I learned in petroleum, translated into award winning leadership, when combined. There is a saying that everyone has one good book in them, this is mine. Thank you for reading.

PART I: Building an Outstanding Leader

I am an outstanding leader, but don't take my word for it. In 2020, Southwest Airlines awarded me that distinguished honor and then again in 2024. If you ask me what I am? I am a leader. I wasn't always comfortable with that. I was never the most confident person, as you read my story, you will understand. Not only have I won awards, but my team has also. My team and I have been asked to assist with various airports and projects, mentorship, you name it. Prior to my airline time, I did a lot of the same in other locations. From bankrupt and broken, to standing in front of the Virginia General Assembly to explain the operation of our facility. As you read on, you will understand that this was not what I thought was in the cards for me.

Validation from Southwest Airlines did a lot for me, but there were years of work, years of struggle, which shaped my journey. Long days, meetings, hours on end studying drawings, sitting in safety meetings, teaching and being taught, training and being trained. These things shaped me, each one. My leadership was developed through failure, in my personal life and professional life. What you see today is a product of 28 years in petroleum, much more than half of my life. I have had the fortune and misfortune of always being around when things went bad, like the arsonist on the fire department. I learned through every one of those events and I want to share those stories with you.

As a manager in my business, we are measured more by the things that don't happen than by the ones that do. Zero spills, zero injuries, zero fuel shortages, zero turnover, zero issues. That is what is expected of me. I have found over the years that when you are good at delivering that, some people can get the impression that the job is easy. Let me be clear, the job is never easy.

The struggles that I faced early in life were likely more than most will face in their entire life. The struggle shaped me. In some ways the struggles hardened me, in other ways unlocked my passion, and compassion as a leader.

Before I get to the part inside of the fence and leadership awards, I need to tell you what happened before I swiped my Amoco Oil Company badge to the petroleum world for the first time.

Chapter One: Can Anyone Hear Me?

I have a vivid memory of being locked in a closet, pitch black, as dark as dark can get. I remember screaming, crying, over and over. In all honesty, I don't know if that was a nightmare or if it happened. I was told later in life that my mother locked me in the closet as a baby and went out and partied while my dad worked. I know that I was left alone on many occasions as a baby, in a closet or in a crib, it didn't really matter in my nightmares. Despite all of that, I grew up in a loving home, it was just a different home than I would have thought. I wasn't born Luis Graham Martinez; I was born Lewis Graham Brown the 3rd.

My birth mother made sure that my entry into the world would be a rough one. I found out a little later in life that she drank castor oil so that I would be born prematurely, to ensure I would have the same March 10th birthday as my sister. My birth mother dropped me off in a car carrier at my new parent's house and said, "you can have him, I don't want him." It took them a lot of money and more than 2 years of unannounced inspections by child welfare services to adopt me. Unfortunately, my lungs didn't fully develop, so I have struggled with severe asthma for my entire life. I was adopted by my aunt and uncle, Luis and Susan Martinez, my parents. It is tough on you emotionally when you are adopted, I have argued with my mom over these very words. If you weren't, you cannot feel that feeling. That is my experience, no one can tell me what that feels like, it is mine. When you are a kid, you just think, why me? My family was half Puerto Rican, I spent most of my life hoping that people wouldn't ask me why I didn't look like everyone else in my family, it still happens.

As much as I wanted to believe that every time I got in trouble as a kid was because I was adopted, it wasn't. I wanted to rebel; I wanted to push it and then use that as a crutch when I got in trouble.

    Because of my asthma, while most kids went out and played, I had to worry about smoke, dust, and anything else that could cause an attack. I spent more than a few days in the ER on oxygen and struggling to breathe, there isn't a much worse feeling than that. Pills, inhalers, and shots were a part of my regimen growing up. I always wondered why I was made to struggle. There were a few times when I was gasping for air, that I didn't know if I could get the next breath. Because of how sick I was, I couldn't have carpet in my room because of the dust. Between the medicine, the doctor's visits, and the special accommodations, I was an expensive kid. I wouldn't say that we grew up poor, we had everything we needed, but there wasn't a lot extra. When we went to the book fair at school, occasionally, we could buy something but not as much as most. Who needed that junk anyway? To this day, I can't stand the sight of baked chicken, it was a staple on our limited menu.

    My dad worked at Dow-Badische, working shift work during my childhood. My grandfather worked there before him, my uncle and biological father worked there, it was a good blue-collar job in a chemical factory. We had one vehicle, my mom would wake us all up at 10 pm on a school night, so that we could make the 45-minute drive to Williamsburg, Virginia to pick up my dad. Most of the time we slept on the ride, sometimes we didn't. While we waited for my dad to come out, we played I-Spy in the parking lot, i.e. I spy something green. At some point we acquired a second vehicle, a Datsun pickup truck with a cap on the back. My brothers and I spent a lot of days freezing while riding in the back of that, a poor man's minivan. I am pretty sure we absorbed a lot of carbon monoxide back there, but we survived. We also had a 1967 Chevy II Nova before that; it had a hole in the floorboard in the back which enabled us to watch the road as we drove on it. Mom and dad always made ends meet. We always had that new bike at Christmas, a Nintendo to share, and food on the table. As I said, we weren't poor but close to it, my asthma didn't help with the doctors' visits, I am sure.

As if being lower middle class, adopted, with asthma wasn't enough, I was bullied and made fun of quite a bit as a kid. I had curly hair, when it wasn't cut it formed a nice afro. So here I was in elementary school, a white kid with a Puerto Rican name and an afro. It so happened that my name was Graham, which at recess was condensed down to Kill-a-Graham. I spent much of my time on the playground running, hey at least it made me tough and kept me in shape. I went through my younger years and schooling not being the coolest kid.

    I was hyper-active, couldn't sit still. My teachers remembered my energy level, with more than one threatening to "tie me to the chair." My daughter went to the same elementary school as I had before her. When we went for parent teacher day more than twenty years later, the gym teacher Ms. Downey said, and I quote, "I don't remember a lot of the kids, but I remember you." I don't think she meant it as a compliment. Me and my afro played middle school basketball, I wasn't the best on the team, but I could hold my own. I was in the band, playing some trombone. I took 3rd place in the 7th grade talent show dancing and lip syncing to the song "Rumors". I can't say middle school was as bad as elementary school, things seemed to be a little cooler.

As I moved to 8th grade, I tried out for the football team. My big brother was a wide receiver, and I wanted to follow him. One day at practice I hurt my foot badly, I was sure it was broken, and I convinced myself that it was. I had x-rays and it turned out that it wasn't, but I quit anyway. Football was hard, practice was hard, and I wanted the glory of playing but figured out quickly that I didn't want to volunteer for the punishment and discipline that came with it. My dad doesn't know this, but he said something to me when I quit that I have never forgotten to this day. His powerful words spoken in the most deliberate tone, "once a quitter, always a quitter." Wow, profound to say the least. I had disappointed him.

We moved to Newport News, Virginia in my ninth-grade year where I could have a clean slate and a fresh start. It was great, nobody knew me. My dad worked at the Amoco Oil Refinery now and as a family, we were doing much better. We lived in a nice townhouse, even though it was more than five miles, I rode my bike to school most days. I enjoyed the freedom and really felt like it was a fresh start. I played JV football in the 10th grade, by and large I enjoyed it and hung in there, I wasn't a quitter, and I was going to prove it. I had all the talent and ability, but I didn't make the effort to shine. Just being good enough, was good enough. That was the last sport I played in high school. I barely got by in school and didn't have the grades for it even if I wanted to play. I was more interested in hanging out with my friends, partying, and finding trouble when it was available. As I was usually the class clown, I made plenty of friends. By the time I was in 11th grade, my friends and I would disappear for lunch at school, drink, smoke, go back to school, and then head out to find more trouble. I wasn't always looking for a fight, but I never walked away from one either. In 11th grade, my friend Ronald was getting picked on and came to me looking for help. I waited until we were between classes and grabbed the guy by his shirt collar, held him up against the locker and said, if you are looking for a fight, let's fight. He stuttered and stumbled over his words, saying, "I'll meet you after school." I responded with, I am here right now. He didn't want to fight, and the teachers were rushing to us, so I ducked back in the crowd and off to class I went.

    Not long after, I was with my friend Mike and we went with our friends Ivan and Omar, over to a girl named Beth's house. We were sitting in the living room when seven guys from neighboring Menchville High School walked in. Beth was dating one of them or whatever the case was, but they were looking for a fight. One of the guys had a gun. They walked around the room, pushing my friends on their heads. I had already decided when they got to me, I was swinging, and I did. I got one good shot off, that was the last thing I remember. When it was over, I was beaten badly. Bloody, black eyes, and a headache for days. I dated a girl in high school named Paula who lived in my neighborhood, her parents were both Newport News Police Officers. I went to their house, her mom took a bunch of pictures of me and wrote a report, but nothing ever came of it. For better or for worse, I guess you could say I wouldn't back down to anyone.

    Some of those same people were around for another incident that took place, though I hate to call it that. This was more of a wrong place at the wrong time situation. As we were hanging out at my friend Mike's one night, someone was hanging out at the house that I didn't particularly like. I basically lived there on the weekends; it wasn't uncommon for us to have 10 to 20 people over. On this occasion, we had all been drinking and I decided it was best to take a walk to get away from the person, a girl I had previously dated I believe. As I walked around the block, I noticed there was spray paint on many of the cars that were parked on the street. As I kept walking, people were coming out of their houses and onto the street to see their cars. An angry mob began to form behind me as I walked, and I put together that these people thought I had done it. I kept walking and as I got to a three-way intersection, I was commanded to put my hands up by the Newport News Police, who were now surrounding me on all sides. I complied. Suddenly like an angel in the night, a familiar voice. My friend's mom said, "Graham, is that you?" I said, yes, it is. In her best angry mom voice she yelled, "get over here." Again, I complied. I got in the back of the police car; the same one I used to ride to school in occasionally with her and my friend. She checked my hands for paint, there was none. She asked me where I was coming from and when I gave her the address, I could see her disappointment.

    The address was well known to them, not like we were doing anything bad; we just made a lot of noise. As we pulled up, she gave me the breathalyzer, which I failed. She could see my friends peeking out of the windows. Her last words to me that night, "you go back in there and don't come back out, tell your friends that if I see another one in the window after you go in, I am going to pull all of you out of there." I heard her words loud and clear, when I got inside, I yelled, everyone away from the windows. That was the last of my troubles for the night. I sure was lucky she was there, that was the one and only time I have ever been in the back of a police car.

I soon met my future wife and subsequently, ex-wife, we spent most of our senior year dating. One night as I was sleeping at my best friend's house, he snuck away to her house where she slept with him, heartbreaking, I lost a friend and a girlfriend. A month or two later, she stormed into the movie theater where I was watching Pulp Fiction on a date and made a scene. I did not get to watch Pulp Fiction that night, and it took me about 20 years before I finally got around to it. We got back together and graduated high school as a couple, and it was time to move on.

I would be remiss if I did not close this out by saying that if it wasn't for my parents adopting me, there is a good chance I wouldn't be alive today. The care I needed was exhausting and expensive. My entire family sacrificed for me repeatedly, I was blessed beyond imagination. I owe them my life. My mom Susan is one of the most selfless and caring people in the world. I could not have gone to a better home, period. Though I did not know at the time, I was better off. I do not know how they afforded all that we had, but we had a good life, and we were together.

Chapter 1: Key Message(s)

Life isn't fair and it can be dark, it doesn't matter if you deserve it or not. Sleep with one eye open, it could be enlightening.

The book fair wasn't very fair at all when you're broke.

Whether it's a mom, wife, or friend, loyalty can be hard to come by. I learned the value of it in this chapter of my life.

Chapter Two: Bankruptcy, Divorce, and the Roaches

I graduated high school, barely. I didn't have to move out, but I wanted to. I wasn't a school person, and my future wife convinced me that we should move in together, so we did. We moved into a section 8 apartment complex; it was rough. There were times at night that I wouldn't have dared to go outside. I didn't have a phone, I couldn't call for help if I had to, I was flat broke. I worked at Jiffy Lube, and my wife at a restaurant, we had roommates to help with the bills, I couldn't afford it otherwise. My friend helped me buy a 20-gauge single shot shotgun, which was my security system. I suspected the lady that lived across from us was a prostitute and there were usually a lot of guys coming and going. I would look out the window at night and see them leaning on my car, what was I going to do about it? Not a damn thing.

The apartment at Cedar Hill in Newport News, Virginia, had roaches, countless roaches. It was nothing to have one crawling across you when you were sleeping. Food had to be kept in the fridge, it was the only place that was secure. When I eventually moved out of there, I trashed almost everything, I couldn't risk moving the roaches with me.

My girlfriend at that point decided it was time for us to get married, so we did. When I say I had no plans in life, I mean just that. I had no direction, no ambitions, no goals. We lived together, we got married, we struggled together, no other plans needed. The thing about struggling is that sometimes you know you are in it and sometimes you don't. When you are trying to just get through a day, you don't stop and think about the car that just broke down, you just beg and scrap and figure out how to fix it. We had a beautiful wedding surrounded by both of our families at the Amoco Refinery clubhouse, overlooking the York River. That was one of the few highlights of my time with her.

A bit of good news came my way soon, a promotion. I took automotive technician class in high school, and it was a bit of a hobby, or necessity given my limited income. I worked at Jiffy Lube making $7.25 an hour when I was in high school and continued thereafter. One day I was approached by my manager who offered me an assistant manager position if I was willing to move about an hour away to Richmond, Virginia. My wife and I were on our way. I was assistant manager at a brand-new store, and she was working at a Ford dealer, we were doing ok, a little more than making ends meet. That seemed like a good time for us. I bought a brand-new motorcycle, we had a decent apartment, and I was good at my job. I went from assistant manager at one store, to another, to managing a store, to managing a bigger store, twice. My stores performed, of 27 stores in our franchise, we were usually in the top 3 in the metrics. The owners loved me, and I loved them. I eventually managed one of the busiest stores in the Richmond market, at 19-20 years old.

The more money I made, the more my wife spent. I worked a minimum required 50 hours a week, often more. I didn't mind, I was making $50k a year, much more than the $7.25 per hour was getting me. Things were slowly looking up. There was a guy that worked for me who was involved in an unfortunate event in the couple of years before he worked for me. He was an innocent bystander in a convenience store robbery and had been shot. Obviously, he survived, but by all accounts, it affected him a lot. I had a soft spot for him, and I let him move in with us as a roommate, he didn't pay much but it helped pay the bills.

    At that point, things were good, as good as they had been. Our marriage was going ok, and work couldn't have been better, except for the time a few of the guys who worked for me attempted to sabotage my car. When I got promoted initially, the crew thought one of them was going to get the job, so it wasn't well received. Fortunately for me, my sliding glass door in the apartment looked out at the car, watching them turn and run was kind of funny, to be honest. For the first time in my life, I was getting free race tickets with the company, sitting in a suite here and there. Man, it felt good to be "somebody." We bought a Pontiac Firebird with T-tops, I can still see us riding down the interstate in Richmond, listening to those new Green Day songs with the T-tops off. I thought things were good and didn't really have a reason to think otherwise. I knew the struggle, and this was not a struggle.

    It was short lived before things began to unravel again. My wife was spending quite a bit of time at work and quite a bit of money on my credit card and my employee/ roommate was staying up late, on the phone. As she became more distant, I figured out quickly that she was cheating on me. I confirmed that with a note I found in her purse, expressing her love for one of the married guys she worked with. This was a tough pill to swallow, for the second time. I was too broke to leave, it was a difficult position to be in. I had to go to work and lead people, it was tough. One day, I came home to check the mail and pulled a phone bill out that was close to a solid inch thick. I opened it to find $1,200 dollars' worth of late-night calls to 900 numbers, it was my roommate. I didn't have $1,200 and I couldn't even dream of getting a loan for that much. On top of that, she had just purchased a brand-new set of tires for her boyfriend's car. My mom paid the phone bill for me, that hurt having to spend their money on that. I remember having to take my mom's credit card from the restaurant she worked at to go to the atm and take a cash advance, it was so painful, and shameful.

Things were falling apart. I lost all trust in people; it seemed as if everyone in my life that I trusted would eventually betray me, except my family. I would sit around thinking that I wasn't even 21 yet and I had been adopted, born prematurely, cheated on, and I had nothing left. Failure to launch.

It became clear to me that I needed to get out and get out I did. While my wife was at work, I packed up everything I could in my car. I told my boss I was moving back home, an hour away. I was hopeful that they could accommodate me at a local store in the Tidewater, Virginia area, and they did. I called her and said I was leaving; you figure it out. I didn't have money to file bankruptcy, my parents helped me. I didn't have money to file for divorce, so again my parents helped me. None of that really mattered to me, I was going home. I had been out of the house for a couple of years, it was strange going home. I started to receive default notices, bills, and more bills. One day she called me to come pick up a bill from her at her new job at a rental car counter at the Newport News airport. I didn't know that she too had moved back. When I picked up that bill, she seemed happy to tell me that she was now dating my other best friend, the one friend that I had when I moved back. He and I spent a lot of time together, I stayed at his place a lot, now that was gone. I was down two friends and one wife.

I ended up at court in Richmond, Virginia over the apartment lease, she had not paid it and defaulted on it. I requested that the court split the debt up and let me make payments on my half, since I was half of the lease. I said right there for all to hear in court with her standing next to me, that she cheated on me and I had no choice. The judge replied in a compassionate way, that unfortunately it didn't work that way, I was on the lease I was responsible for all of it. The representative from the leasing agency for the apartment stopped me just as I walked out of the courtroom, to paraphrase he said "hey, I'm sorry for what you are going through, and I wish I could do something, but my hands are tied." I said, I get it. I will be filing for bankruptcy, and so it went. I remember sitting at the place I went to file bankruptcy, as low as low could be. I didn't really understand where I went wrong, why me? I just couldn't grasp it. Soon after, I found myself with a divorce attorney. Divorce was done, the debt was gone, along with my credit. I would say I lost self-esteem, but I didn't have any. I didn't care about anything, anymore. My life was a cascade of failures.

I was 21 years old, living with my parents. High school education and nothing to offer the world. I didn't care, what did it matter? Everything I did in life failed, and I was a failure. I was working at Jiffy Lube again, I didn't want to be in management anymore, I felt hopeless, and I couldn't deal with the stress and people, why should I? I had been so good at it and now I just didn't care. Though I didn't want it, I was persuaded to step back into management. My head wasn't in it and after being verbally abused by the manager more than a few times, I resigned. My mom and dad owned a restaurant, which was about 5 miles away. I called the Jiffy Lube district manager, thanked him for the opportunities the company had given me, I told him I was done. I walked the 5 miles to my parents' restaurant, again, wondering where I went wrong. I went to work at a Chrysler dealership where I didn't have enough tools to be an effective mechanic. I made some friends and most of the time barely met the 25-hour minimum for labor hours turned, I just didn't have the equipment or the drive, if I am being honest. This is the point I thought, I am at the bottom. If you have never been to the bottom, you can't understand the gravity of those words. My life was all struggle, with a side of my parents bailing me out, constantly. They were my guardian angels, if it wasn't for them, I would have given up on life, but they never gave up on me.

    My time alone was short lived. A few months after I moved back home, I had a surprise when I found out my new girlfriend and future wife, was pregnant. My first thought, I don't even have a place to live. I was in real trouble. I stepped out of one difficult situation and set myself up for another. I really wasn't sure how I was going to afford to feed a baby, much less a family. I couldn't blame this on anyone, this one was on me. Of course, sometimes these things can be a blessing in disguise. I was living a reckless life at this point, headed for trouble. I was drinking anytime I could, I smoked cigarettes, if you will remember earlier, my lungs weren't exactly in the best shape for that. I didn't care, I didn't care about tomorrow or today for that matter, I had thrown in the towel. I had a daughter on the way, and I didn't have time to feel sorry for myself anymore, I had to figure things out quickly. One day my dad came to me while I was living back at home and said the refinery is hiring operators. I didn't know what an operator was, and my dad wasn't the best communicator. So, his description was you turn valves and check pressures, which meant absolutely nothing to me. He told me to apply for the job, so I did. Weeks later I walked into a panel interview surrounded by seven folks. They asked me safety questions; I was well versed in these having previously managed at Jiffy Lube. I had no pressure on me in the interview anyway, I didn't expect anything to come from it and I honestly didn't care.

One night a few weeks after the interview, I drove down to the Yorktown Fishing Pier, it had a prime view of the city like skyline of the refinery and the power plant next door. I had no idea what went on there, but I knew I needed to get in. I knew this could be the chance I needed, and I sure needed it. Reality hit me; something has got to give. So, I said the prayer. I looked out over the water towards the refinery, and I said the prayer. Now whether you believe in prayer or not, that is up to you. The prayer I said went something like this,

"Dear Lord, I have never asked for anything. I need this. I need this to feed my daughter. Please let me get this job and I swear I will make the most of it. Please Lord, Amen."

A few weeks later, my prayer was answered. I got the call to come in for my physical and I got the job offer to start on October the 4th, 1997. I was making $13.16 per hour, I hit the lottery. One of the most rewarding parts of this was when I went to visit my grandfather and tell him I got the job, he was so proud of me. I started in October, and

Martinez- On the Other Side of the Fence

he passed away on December the 13th, just two months later. I was very close with him and devastated. He knew I made it before he died, he was proud of me, and he told me so. I was thankful that he passed away knowing that, and I know he is proud of me in heaven now. Amoco, here I come.

Chapter 2: Key Message(s)

Sometimes kindness doesn't pay, but it shouldn't keep you from doing what you think is right. Sometimes things just don't work out, but that's a reflection of them, not you.

When all else fails, say a prayer. You never know, it just might help.

What do you talk about for $1200 dollars, and to think that I touched that phone.

I learned the value of trust, and how hard it can be to get it back when it's lost.

PART II: The Refined Life

A new chapter in my life began and I had no idea just where it would take me. At 21 years old, I couldn't begin to comprehend the magnitude of the impact this would have on my life. I would report to work each day, enter the gates of a city within a city. I felt important, like a part of something. I was behind the gates, inside the fence. The refinery was a world to itself, like sovereign territory. I didn't leave that place for the next 21 years.

There were noises, there were smells, machinery, big and small. The flare, which burned off gases and served as an emergency outlet, glowed, day and night, year after year, without fail. There were ships, railcars, tugboats, trucks, there was something moving in every direction possible, constant motion. It was like learning to walk again. There were names for various fuels and components that most people have never heard of, the same with the equipment. There were fires, big ones. There were spills. It seemed on any given day I went to work; I could encounter anything. To this day, I get hungry at 11:30, when the steam whistle used to blow, alerting us to lunchtime. After so many years of programming, it just becomes the norm. The other unmistakable sound, the evacuation siren. If it was noon on Wednesday, without fail, you would hear the following come across the plant radio "This is K-I-L-3-2-6, testing the Amoco Yorktown Refinery radio alert system". I can hear "Smedley" the guard, as my coworker Willy Owens used to call him, his distinct voice calling it out. That was followed by an air raid siren that could be heard for miles. If you heard that sound, and it wasn't noon, on

Wednesday, that was an indication something bad had happened or was getting ready to.

Without further ado, let's get into it.

Chapter Three: The Refinery Smells Like Money

I had it easy. Fortunately, my dad worked in the refinery, and I knew many people that I went on to work with. I was pretty good at softball and played with the refinery team prior to working there, I felt at home and welcomed because of that. Amoco had two teams, the Ultimate and Silver, aptly named after our gasoline products. Before I started working there but as I understood it, the Ultimate team chose who they wanted, leaving the rest of us on the scrap heap. I feel like we beat them as much as they beat us, so I don't think their plan worked very well. The cool thing about the refinery and the reason I added that bit, is to illustrate the social connection. We were one big family that I was now a part of, and I was sure proud to pull that Amoco Silver jersey on.

The refinery was a lot like the military, at least I think so. We had our own basic training, called B.O.T.S. Before we could be set free in the world, we endured several weeks of that. We didn't know which unit we would be assigned to, so we got trained for any eventual destination. A few other people in my class had personal connections like I did, everyone lobbied for one place or the other based on where their family or friends worked. As I sat in basic training only 3 days in, we looked out of the window of our training trailer located next to the main gate to the sight of black smoke and flames. Wow, what kind of place is this? The Cat Cracker was going into turnaround and the fractionator tower, at least as I remember it, had a fire in the bottom. It wasn't the worst fire, small as refinery fires go.

Following basic training and much like the softball teams, there was a draft hierarchy, whereas the people that were thought to be smart would go to the process units. Dummies like me, we went to Oil Movements. Oil Movements was where the physical work was done, the logistics. We docked the ships, loaded, and unloaded rail cars, climbed those big tanks. We did that work no matter the weather. Hot, cold, day, night, snow, ice, we were out there. The tradeoff was, we had freedom. We had free reign over the entire refinery complex. We could get in our trucks and if we were lucky, turn on the radio, and head out. The process unit folks, had it easy, most of the time, at least that is the way it was always explained to me. The SIGNIFICANT difference being, when things went bad, they were in a bomb factory. Their job was to keep all the fuel that was being refined, in the pipes and towers. They had to ensure it was flowing at the right temperature, the right pressure, and to the right place. When they didn't do those things just right, BOOM.

I went to Oil Movements in January and not long after in early March, there was a fire on a coke drum. The coker was a unit with four very large drums, a few hundred feet tall each. The purpose of the coker was to take all the products that could not be used for anything else, including some wastewater sludge that was injected, and making it into petroleum coke. Petroleum coke looks like coal, if you saw it in a train car, you likely wouldn't know the difference. The coker heats this material up to many hundreds of degrees and bakes it as solid as a rock. Then a decoker comes in and with extremely high-water pressure, cuts it out of the drum into a sluiceway below, then loaded by tractors onto a waiting railcar. Pet Coke, as it was called, was not a clean burning fuel source. In the early days of the refinery, it was shipped next door to the power plant to be blended with their coal. In my time, it was shipped overseas, as I remember it.

    On the night of the fire, one of the drums developed a crack, leading to a fire. I was three months into my refinery career when I got the call to come assist, so I did. There was an industrial elevator that you could ride to the top, unfortunately you couldn't use that during a fire, so up the stairs I went. Once I got to the fire, I was given my instructions, stand here, hold this fire hose on this fire, easy enough. I was told that they were in this process of emptying or depressuring the drum, so I just had to keep it wet until then. It was roughly 2am, surrounded by deafening noise, the structure shaking, and I was just standing there with the hose leaning on a handrail. At first it was a little scary, but after a while, just boring. I still have a laminated copy of the email that was sent to me and a few others, thanking us for our participation, I believe we also received 10 dollars in Amoco gas coupons, that won't get you far these days. That email from 1998 is one of the first work emails I ever received. That was also my first refinery fire, but it certainly wouldn't be the last.

    I worked overtime, as much as possible. I learned every job I could and got qualified to work all the positions in my department. I wouldn't be denied. I had my chance, and I wasn't going to waste it. I was part of "A" shift, I was part of something. We worked together; we spent a lot of time together. Many nights of philosophical and religious debates in the control room at 3am, anything to stay awake.

Harold Johnson tried to kill me twice, I still remind him occasionally. One night he threw a pipe fitting into the back of our truck while I was trying to grab my gloves from the floor, the pipe bounced off the plastic bedliner, through the window, and right to my ribs. Thankfully, it was winter, and I had a lot of clothes on. We had to fabricate a story that he threw a steam hose in the back and a fitting went through the window. Well, he had to, I just had to remain silent.

    The second close call with Harold was when we were out dealing with some freezing weather, and we were trying to get a steam hose flowing to thaw out some large water pipes. As he moved the hose, it snapped and started blowing steam everywhere. I was as blind as could be, surrounded by pipes and a steam cloud. The best way to describe it is looking out of an airplane window when you are flying through a cloud, except the cloud was in the plane too. By luck and memory, I was able to escape the blowing steam hose and piping, unscathed. I told Harold that was twice, and we didn't need a third.

    A little about our refinery, it was small as far as refineries go. We refined about 62,000 barrels of oil every day, that's about 2.6 million gallons each day. Refined means that we would take raw crude oil and refine it through various methods, into gasoline, diesel, jet fuel, kerosene, propane, butane, and other products. That fuel supplied the local market and various east coast ports. The crude oil that was processed came from all over the world. Each night at midnight, we made a crude feed tank switch, the oil that was going to be processed that day. The crude oil was not just any crude oil. That oil came from all over the globe, depending on what the characteristics were and what the cost was. At midnight, we would input our recipe for the crude blend that was provided to us by economics and scheduling, and we would get to work. we would blend the heaviest gravity crude first, then start bringing in the light. We would pump light crude from the floating suction, that literally floated on the tank top. We pumped the heavy crude from the bottom which was pumped just a few feet from the bottom of the tank.

    The properties of these crude oils had been studied in a crude assay or study of the composition, hand blended in a lab, so that there was a predictable amount of each cut of refined product in them. For example, if you brought in a crude that contained more diesel content, and the economic margins for diesel were good, then you focused on making that. These crudes varied in sulfur and many other factors went into the selection. Ultimately, a refinery is made to operate within a certain range of various parameters of crude, and our job was to make that mixture perfectly. While the product was going in, the finished products coming out had to be sold and moved to their destination. Any upset in the weather or the process could throw the whole delicate balance off. Gasoline was blended the same way as crude oil, and occasionally diesel fuel was as well. We had a full lab, capable of running any required testing that a refinery would need. If there were any deviations to the expected outcome of the product quality, the process unit engineers had to make decisions on how to get it back on track by adjusting temperatures and pressures, or whatever other voodoo those guys did. The chemical engineers were smart guys, I remember sitting in basic training watching them draw hydrocarbon bonds on a board and explaining this stuff to us. I was certainly in a different world.

I joined the Yorktown Refinery Fire Department as soon as I was allowed to, a year or two after I started. I was a little scared when I did, but I think that is why I did it. Some people thought it was crazy to be on the fire department in a refinery, it was. There were a few people on my shift that were on it, to me it was the cool crowd to be in. The thought of going in, when everyone else was running away, just seemed appealing. During the training/try out, there were a few tests that we had to do, to prove that we could handle it. I thought these were simple, honestly, I only remember one of them that stood out. One of the other guys that joined with me, went before I did, and it looked as easy as the rest of the tests. We had to hold a fire hose, with 150 lbs. of water pressure spraying, for four minutes straight. The other guy was a lot bigger than me, more heavyset. He seemed to breeze through it, now it was my turn. About two minutes in, I realized that it wasn't quite as easy as I thought. I didn't want anyone to think I was weak, I held on and tried as much as anything, to make it look like it wasn't hard, but it was, I passed.

Chief Dickie Burroughs sent me to Delaware State Fire School, my first work excursion. It was hot, hard, but fun. We went through drills, the smokehouse, classroom, and I left there certified in basic brigade skills. In a refinery, like any other fire department, there are training requirements due to the liability and danger associated with the job. I also joined the confined space rescue team or CSRT; we trained monthly on both. On the CSRT team, we spent the first 20 minutes tying rescue knots, lifting knots, any knot you may need. The most fun was rappelling. We rappelled from the large storage tanks, more than 50' in the air, or off the process units, even higher. Like many things in life, it got easier once you took the first step. Walking over the edge of a tank or over a handrail can be quite intimidating. The exercise was meant to not only teach us how, but to learn to trust our equipment, and each other. If someone were to be overcome by poisonous gas, or have a medical emergency, we were responsible to gear up and go get them. We didn't have to do that too often, but we would be ready if needed.

The Chief called me over one day to tell me he was sending me to Williams Fire and Hazard school in Beaumont, Texas. I was one of two that were going to attend Advanced Liquid Firefighter school. I was rewarded because of my work in responding to a large fire and it was awesome news. My biggest problem was that I was scared to fly. As I mentioned before, I grew up in a modest income family, we didn't fly. I was 30 years old and had never stepped on a plane, ironic that I would go on to work for the airlines later. I went to Norfolk International Airport, where I boarded a Continental Airlines flight, straight to Houston. I didn't dare move the entire flight. On arrival, we switched to a turboprop and made our way to Beaumont.

On arrival there, we were greeted by old brown wood paneling in the airport, 1980's style. Hurricane Rita* had also devastated that area, just the year before. I had never seen devastation like that. The top floors of the hotel we stayed in were still covered by tarps. Gas station awnings mangled, we made our way to Sabine Pass, where I saw huge fishing boats, sitting in parking lots, where they had landed during the hurricane. There was also a large petroleum tank that had floated off its foundation that found its way to a marsh on the edge of the Gulf of Mexico. I would estimate the tank to be 50,000 to 80,000 barrels. If you think a tank can't float away, I saw it with my own eyes. That was an eye-opening experience, I had never seen that kind of devastation. I was fortunate enough to meet Dwight Williams, the namesake of the company. He is a legend in the industrial firefighting world, having responded to and snuffed out some very large petroleum tank fires and oil well fires during the gulf war. Listening to his stories was an amazing experience and inspired me to want to be a better firefighter. He told us that the fire was a thief, stealing our money, and I always looked at it that way afterwards. It was amazing to be around firefighters from all over the world and I gained valuable experience to take back with me to the refinery. The worst part of that whole experience was when I returned and had to explain the $75 dollar appetizer platter from Pappadeaux's seafood, that my senior travel partner convinced me to purchase. When Chief Burroughs gave you that look, you knew it wasn't good. There was never a fire I was in that was as scary as facing Chief Burroughs that day.

Not all refinery days were bad days, quite the opposite. On a bright and sunny day when all was working well, there was no better place to be. Some of my favorite memories were doing some of the simplest tasks. On Sunday mornings, we were responsible to go out and pull P-4 samples on all our gasoline blend component tanks. For the longest time, I didn't know what the hell P-4 even meant, I just pulled the samples. If I remember correctly, that was the name of the program that was used by the gasoline blender to ensure the blends were made using the right components, to remain on-spec. Gasoline is made up of many different blend components, some with lower vapor pressure, some with higher octane, all combined to meet a government specification for you to buy at the pump. On those beautiful Sunday mornings, I would pull up on the street and park, turn my radio up so that I could hear it as I walked in and out of tank dike walls, and pulled sample after sample. If I didn't have the one truck that had an FM radio, I would just flip over to AM and listen to the local morning fishing show that was on. It's funny how these are the things you remember.

  My other favorite memories were sitting on the dock, loading barges, ships, or fueling tugs. If you came in on afternoon shift, usually that is when the tugs got their fuel. We rolled the hose out, did some paperwork, pulled out a chair, and sat there on the edge of the tug berth, watching the boats, watching the tug guys fish, or reading a magazine. If it was a big tug, it was nothing for us to put twenty thousand gallons or more on. That would take hours, so for hours, I sat and thought to myself that I was getting paid for this. It just didn't get much better. Of course, those were the good days, not the ones where it was freezing, and I was huddled up next to the steam radiator as I waited for it to finish. Those were the best jobs; you weren't stuck on the dock all night. When unloading a large crude tanker, it would be there for two and three days at a time. I would work my 12 hours, go home and sleep, and repeat until it was gone. Since I liked to be busy, sometimes I could convince people to let me have the harder job and they take the gravy. The dock house was small, like a jail cell. There weren't enough magazines, newspapers, or tv shows on your pocket-sized Casio tv, to pass the time. A walk up and down the dock would sometimes produce excitement, a boat with someone smoking under the dock, fish activity, or maybe some random big waves, when there seemed to be nothing around that caused them. Some of us speculated that submarines caused them, coming or going to the Yorktown

Naval Weapons Station, but they usually came through on the surface, so who knows.

Working the Oil Movements console in the refinery (circa 2004)

In December of 2005, I started a new job as the truck terminal operator, a decision that would change my life. When I worked inside of the refinery, I was in a pool of thirty-five personnel. At the truck terminal, there were 2, my boss and me. I took a lot of heat for that from my coworkers. At that point I was making over $100k per year, I worked every overtime that was available to me. At the truck terminal, I would barely get any. I took a $30k per year pay cut. I had no debt though which allowed me to do it, I was smart, especially after being burned by my ex-wife early in life. My son was two years old, and my daughter was seven, I was on shift work prior to the move. From the day I started in the refinery, all I heard was that it was too small, not profitable, and that it would shut down, more on that part later. What I did know was that if it did, I would be more valuable if I knew more jobs than the rest, a move that would pay dividends later.

    I got a lot of exposure at the truck terminal, our commercial folks would visit, they knew me by name. I established a reputation for myself with the truck carriers and the customers, as someone who always answered the call and always kept things moving. I learned skills that helped me throughout the rest of my career, software programming, meter repairs, electronics, list goes on. I am certain that the move to the truck terminal was the launching point for the success I have had in life from then on. My boss Rick retired in 2009, and I assumed the role of Supervisor, someone else from the refinery came to work with me and I taught them what I knew. Eventually they retired, and I brought another in and did the same. I had made a nice niche for myself; things were going well. Best of all, I was home every night and, on the weekends, able to be at the games and weekend events that I had to miss while on shift work. I knew I made the right move.

    I also learned about fuel additives for the first time in my life at the truck terminal. Have you ever wondered what the difference was in one gas station to another? It might not be as much as you think, not even among branded gas stations. For instance, I worked at an Amoco refinery, but it was common for an Exxon truck to load at our load rack. By and large, gasoline is a fungible product, meaning it is generic. Wherever you are geographically, the EPA has designated what gasoline can be sold in that area and what specification it must meet for summer or winter use. It makes no difference who makes the fuel, the difference is in the additive, location, and the season.

The EPA also certifies detergents for gasoline, and if you choose to use a detergent by a certain manufacturer, you must ensure that you comply with what is called the L.A.C., or lowest acceptable concentration. What does that mean? The Environmental Protection Agency determines the amount of detergent needed to keep your engine burning clean, therefore creating less air pollution. With generic gas, at generic stations, and in the case of my terminal's process, there is less additive. Whereas the EPA might say you have to inject 200cc's of additive per 1000 gallons of gas, we would inject roughly 300cc's. This way if there were any issues with your additive injectors, we could be certain that we had enough to stay above the requirement. In the case of the branded stations, they would provide their own proprietary additive, in those cases the L.A.C. was roughly the same, but they would put in three, four, and sometimes five times the amount required. So, if you wonder the next time, you go fill up, why one costs more than another, that's your answer. The additive was very expensive, $40,000 for 4,000 lbs., and that was the price in 2006. I am not a chemist, nor did I ever work in the refinery lab. When people ask me, is it worth it? I can't say for sure one way or the other, I'm not qualified to give an official answer. What I can say, is that if you compare it to your laundry detergent, if the box says one scoop gets your clothes clean and it does, are you going to use four scoops? You can probably get an answer in a chemist's book, only speculation from me.

Chapter 3: Key Message(s)

There is so much out there to learn. Regardless of what you think you know; you have two ears and one mouth for a reason. Listen twice as much as you speak. When opportunity is there, recognize it, take it, and don't waste it.

Fire was a thief and contrary to the song, we did need water and did not let it burn.

Some said the refinery stinks, some said it smelled like money. I think it was both.

In this chapter I learned that in the words of Socrates, "all I know, is that I know nothing"

(3) *Hurricane Rita was the strongest hurricane to strike Southeast Texas and Southwest Louisiana since Hurricane Audrey on June 27, 1957 (Source National Weather Service https://www.weather.gov/lch/rita_main)*

Chapter Four: This Place Was Lit

Above I mentioned the good days, there were many. There were also more than a few bad days. Below is a collection of firsthand accounts of some of the worst days in the history of the Yorktown Refinery. These stories are based on my experience and a story of a fatality from a newspaper report, referenced later. Of course, many others have many stories to tell, I couldn't possibly know them all, only my experience and information that I heard from my own conversations. Full disclosure, I never worked on the refinery process units, my understanding of those processes is limited to secondhand knowledge.

On June 6th, 2001, at around 6:30 pm, the sky lit up. Every refinery worker's nightmare. This was the first time in my life that I had ever seen or heard of anything like this, it was sobering. During a severe thunderstorm, lightning struck the Ultraformer, or near it. The Ultraformer is a high pressure, high temperature, gas processing unit, and a dangerous one. Though I wasn't in the fire department yet, we had to scramble to close valves on tanks and watch as the entire unit burned. Seeing the refinery on fire is not something that is easy to describe in words. It took a few hours to put this one out and thankfully no one was seriously injured. The conclusion was that the vibration from the strike caused something to leak flammable gas under high pressure, leading to the fire. Though it took about a year to rebuild that unit, the refinery continued to run and the product from that unit to make gasoline was replaced by purchasing components on the open market and imported in. No one was severely injured but there were some minor injuries, and I believe a few of the responders suffered permanent hearing damage from the incredible noise levels during their response. I spoke to a few of my coworkers that responded to this, they were scared. They were not sure that they should have been in the areas that they were in, I would come to understand that feeling in a few short years.

The Thanksgiving Night Fire

(4)

The big Thanksgiving night fire happened in 2005, just after midnight at 12:57am. This was the first "real fire" I was directly involved in. I was on "C" shift now and we had decided that we would do a breakfast that night for Thanksgiving. Every night at midnight, there were tasks to be done, including the crude feed tank switch. I was a step-up supervisor that night and as it was a holiday, we were on a skeleton crew. As I pulled the door open to the control room to go in for breakfast, the sky turned orange. I knew what it was, and it could only be one thing. The radios started going off with comments such as, "the Combo is on fire", "the Combo blew up", "everyone over there is probably dead". I was the offsite supervisor, meaning I was the incident commander, to the firehouse I went. I notified security to call out everyone you can. It was sheer chaos.

As I arrived at the firehouse a minute or two later, there were only three of us to respond, Mike Lentz, Willy Owens, and me. Mike instructed me to wait for York County to arrive, whose station was right down the street and who provided us with mutual aid. Mike and Willy took Engine 2 and were on their way. I waited a minute or two for the county, and when they arrived, I asked them to follow me to which they agreed. Mike instructed me to take the west side of the unit, while they were on the east. I was driving a rescue truck, loaded with air packs and a mobile command center, no water or pump. As I stepped out and looked behind me, I realized I was alone. I ran back to the corner and looked down the street I had just driven down, the York County engine stopped about 2 blocks down and that was where they sat. I made my way back to them in the rescue truck, they advised me that they would not be joining us until their officers arrived, we were on our own.

I left the truck there and ran on foot, in my heavy firefighter bunker gear to engine 2 and my fellow firefighters. As I was running into the fire, I was nearly certain that this would be my last night on earth. All I could think about were my kids and the fact that my 2-year-old son would never know who I was, it was bad, and I didn't know if this would be the end. We had a 2,000 gallon per minute pump and a remote-control deck gun. There was fire all around us. The air handler and other parts on the roof of the control room were burning next to us, the grass in the pipe alley next to us was burning under the pipes. The tower next to us had a pipe that blew out and it was blowing fire out like a blowtorch. Mike instructed me to put out the pipe alley fire, I protested a bit, but he was right, we were nearly surrounded, and we needed to start somewhere to work the fire away from us. It was cold, 22 degrees. Mike was as big as a bear, his nickname was Bear Paw, I felt confident in his leadership and stayed close to him. I knew that he had been there before, he was a seasoned veteran and someone I trusted. He wouldn't let anything happen to us, at least nothing in our control.

A few minutes later, Mike asked me to go to the firehouse and bring back another portable monitor, so I ran on foot again a few blocks to the firehouse, still in full gear. When I got there, we had a few other firefighters show up, we had help. As I mentioned, it was cold. The overspray from York County's Ladder 1 was coating my squirt truck with ice, along with a layer of ice on my bunker gear. We were moving over 10,000 gallons per minute of water, straight from the York River. Because of the flow, we were dislodging all the marine growth in the system, subsequently plugging the strainers in our fire apparatus. We would then have to take our fire gloves off, disconnect the 5" supply hose, and clean the debris out with our hands. Our fingers were numb, it was pure misery.

Martinez- On the Other Side of the Fence

This fire took us thirteen hours to extinguish. At the end, we lined up fifteen separate 150lb wheeled fire extinguishers, Travis Manry and I would man each end of our semi-circle and begin emptying those into the water stream that was directed at the last bit of the fire. It was finally over. By the time I got back to the firehouse I was beyond tired. I did take time to call home that morning, I knew it would be all over the local news and I didn't want anyone to worry. Not long after the event, we had a post incident review, a hot wash if you will. It wasn't until a few weeks after that we would come to realize that there was asbestos packed into the treads of the fire engine tires that we were meeting next to in the firehouse. The pictures of destruction afterwards looked like something out of a Hollywood movie. Mangled and twisted steel, towers leaning, damage beyond comprehension. Thankfully, again, no one was seriously injured.

The Ultra Low Sulfur Diesel Unit Fire

(5)

Martinez- On the Other Side of the Fence

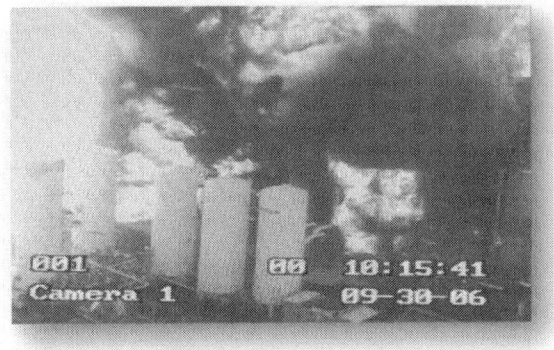

Only ten very short months later, we got the call again. September 30, 2006, at around 10:30 am on a nice Saturday morning, another explosion. I was at home when my pager went off, yes it was a while ago. As I walked out of my front door to look towards the refinery, which was more than ten miles away, there was a mushroom cloud like a bomb had been dropped. The local news reported that the cloud could be seen from the outer banks of North Carolina, 90 miles away. I made my way to the refinery, which was about a 15-minute drive, as I arrived at one of the cross streets, the York County Sheriff's Office had closed the roads and were turning people around, I identified myself as a responder and they let me pass. When I arrived, there were a handful of people on-scene already, so I just jumped into the action. The new ultra-low sulfur diesel processing unit, or ULSD for short, had exploded. There was some operational change made, which caused tubes to overheat in the furnace, and when they finally got too hot, boom.

Later that day I saw myself on the news from the helicopter vantage point, as WAVY-10 was flying overhead during the event. I was manning a smaller portable monitor called a Blitz Fire, my crew and I would slowly work our way towards the furnace as the fuel continued to burn off. We were knee deep in the containment for the unit, which is meant to keep the liquid pool on the unit so that a foam blanket can form in the event of a fire. We snuffed this one out in a matter of a few hours, nowhere near as bad as the one the year before, but a good portion of the unit was destroyed. When I got back to the firehouse to take my gear off, my legs had an oil line past my knees where I had been in the liquid pool with the oil, water, and foam. That was the last major fire I saw in my time in the refinery, though far from the last incident.

Tank 901- The Horton Spheroid

In 2001, we came very close to another catastrophe, nearly over-pressuring a tank containing highly toxic fuel, in the refinery known as light slop. The tank I am referring to was called a Horton Spheroid and it was shaped like a big onion that was supposed to operate at 5-6 psi. Light slop, loaded with thousands of parts per million of hydrogen sulfide, was stored inside. Light slop was aptly named because it was a combination of off-spec products that were stored in tank 700 and 901, to be slowly injected back into the refining stream. Per the Occupational Safety Health Administration [2], at 700 to 1000 parts per million, hydrogen sulfide is fatal within two breaths. In the firehouse we had a radius map showing how far the impact would go if there was a major release from this tank, it could have killed people for several miles in any direction the wind was blowing. H2S as it is known, is a byproduct of refining, sewer gases, and other processes. It is one of the most dangerous substances in industry, one that requires extreme caution.

    I was working at the water treatment plant in the refinery that day, listening to radio chatter from my coworkers. They were discussing high pressure on the tank, Tank 901. They didn't seem certain because of the number being so high, so they went to inspect the tank. On arrival they found a pressure gauge in the pipe alley on the vapor relief line on the tank showing 35 psi, a number that was too high to believe. They also detected the strong odor of H2S, which was certainly not normal. Following that, they climbed up to the top of the tank to check the pressure gauge on top, also 35 psi. This was suddenly a major emergency, with the potential to be catastrophic. The tank was designed to relieve to the flare system at 6.5 psi, that failed. After that, the tank was designed to relieve the atmosphere at ~11 psi, to prevent rupture of the tank, that also failed. At this point the emergency management teams were all involved, and the decision was made to slowly start bleeding the tank off to the flare. It was in the middle of a bright sunny day, and as they opened the tank to the flare, the sky turned black from the smoke. Fortunately, the tank didn't rupture but it had developed a crack in the floor, which caused the smell. We were able to burn the pressure off in a controlled manner. No one was hurt.

    So, what caused this? Unacknowledged alarms. The high-pressure alarm on the tank repeatedly came in, it was ignored, and it was almost catastrophic. Something so simple, one tiny little ½ inch or ¾ inch valve. A few days before the high pressure, there was maintenance work going on in a pipe alley, well away from tank 901. To facilitate that work, mechanics disconnected instrument air that supplied the control valve, which regulated the pressure on tank 901. The valve was set to maintain under the 6.5 psi threshold and allow it to slowly vent to the tank. Of course, in hindsight the valves should have been marked, tagged, and labeled. Assumptions were made, mechanics who did not understand the consequences of utilizing that valve, disconnected a critical piece of equipment. Because of the unacknowledged alarms, combined with the mechanic's decision and the fact that there was not a job safety analysis or work permit done, could have killed at the least dozens of people. It happens that quickly, and that easily.

    I was also on duty the day that the welders went inside to repair the crack in the floor of the tank that developed because of the overpressure. I was responsible for taking a gas detector/ tester into the tank, to verify the reading of oxygen, lower explosive limit, hydrogen sulfide, and carbon monoxide, were all at a level that were permittable for entry and for welding. We were inside of the tank, there was lighting and there was one 24" manway, to crawl in and out of. I was in pretty good shape back then and I estimated that if something happened, I could cover ground quicker than the two welders, to get to the hole first. Fortunately, all went well, and I didn't need to. Had there been an issue, none of us would have gotten out anyway.

    Our plant manager at the time was a guy by the name of Don Parus, he came in and lectured everyone on how close we were to disaster, he told one of our guys how he should be thanking his lucky stars. I don't think he knew that we found the problem; we didn't create it. I was young and ignorant, or inexperienced at the time. I knew it was bad; I knew what happened, but for the most part this was all new to me. We had a major explosion around that time that I also referenced earlier, these two events happened during our short tenure with BP after they purchased Amoco. A couple of years later, this plant manager would go on to bigger and better, taking over the Texas City Refinery. Not long after, there was a major explosion there in 2005 that killed 12 people and injured countless more.

Another incident that took place on the Ultraformer Unit almost cost us one of our own. I was not there when this happened, but I knew this guy well, with him being on our softball team even before I started at the refinery. One night during freezing weather, he was out making a round on the unit, when he identified an issue. A line was plugged and there was a sight glass to see if there was flow going through the pipe. As he tried to free the line to allow flow, the sight glass exploded with shrapnel entering his body. Thankfully someone heard him on the radio and went out to find him, that saved his life. Paramedics responded and were able to get him to a hospital, as I remember it, he was in ICU for quite some time, and I went to visit him a few times. I didn't get to keep up with him much after this, but he did recover and make it back to work. I always enjoyed being around him, I was thankful that he recovered.

In 2016, I responded to an emergency callout regarding a tank overflow. At this point, the refinery had long been shut down and we were in the terminal business. While offloading an oceangoing tanker, multiple alarms came into the control room that went ignored. Not long after, there was a large spill with an 80,000-barrel tank overflowing volatile gasoline blend stock. The emergency response team was activated and responded, deployed fire engines and large portable fire monitors, capable of flowing up to 8,000 gallons per minute. We applied a foam blanket to the gasoline that had breached the tank to suppress vapors. As luck would have it that cold January night, the wind direction was blowing away from populated areas out to the York River. Once the situation was stable, we were able to plan how we would bring the level under control and begin transferring to another tank, we had to be careful not to shift large steel tank components that could have caused a fire and massive gasoline explosion.

In a petroleum tank there are multiple levels of redundancy to prevent these things. High level switches, high-high level switches. These are attached to alarms and alarms, all of which should be tested and verified routinely. I responded to the site of tens of thousands of gallons of gasoline in the dike wall, while the alarms had been repeatedly alerting the control room to an issue. Why didn't they act on them? At the time, there was no work order process for reporting issues, nuisance alarms were constantly coming in and being ignored. In the case of this overflow, there were systematic failures from top to bottom. Poor decisions were made, and those decisions contradicted everything that I had ever been trained to do in that situation. In my experience, there is usually not one thing that fails, there are multiple levels of failure that lead to undesired consequences. In this case, I had to implement approximately twenty actions items when I assumed the facility manager position shortly after the event. There were also a few that lost employment over that incident, it was ugly but fortunately didn't result in a fire.

I have been involved in more events than I can remember, but a few others I want to share will highlight how easily things can turn fatal in a refinery. On two separate occasions, I have been involved in one way or another with mechanics cutting into the wrong pipe, while doing maintenance. On the first occasion, I was sitting in the control room and received a call on the radio from one of the refinery pipefitters, telling me that he thinks he cut into the wrong pipe. I asked him to tell me if he could find a pipe number, and he did, L-804. The 804-line as we referred to it, was called a flare line. That line was a common line that tied all the pressure vessels in the refinery together, to route the vapors on the top of the tanks to be burned off. The line was explosive vapor, on its way to be safely burned. Operations had gone out, walked the job down, tied a green ribbon on the line that the mechanics were to cut. Unfortunately, they cut the next one over in the pipe alley. I didn't believe it when they told me which line it was, I thought if it was that line, they would be dead. I called my supervisor, and he responded to confirm it was. Somehow, the line didn't explode, nothing happened. Either the vapors were too rich, or they were just insanely lucky, but we clamped the line and moved on. Several years later when I was in charge of the terminal, we had a similar incident on a dock line that was being welded on, again the line was identified, **and an operator was standing by** at the end of the line, the mechanics began to cut the wrong line again. It was a bit of a miracle that nothing happened in either case, but this highlights the importance of procedures and labeling, yet again.

    I knew of one fatality in the history of the refinery that I was informed of when I started, George Brannigan. I am including the details of this because this information is readily available to the public. I have heard word of mouth stories, but this information came directly from a 1990 news article from the Los Angeles Times. In May of 1988,

George Branigan who worked for the refinery, died when a spark from a gas compressor ignited a pool of naphtha that he was washing into a process sewer drain nearby. As I understand it, George died only days later, succumbing to his burns.

As the LA times reports [1], he was part of a group of employees that had complained about this process just a few months before, while also proposing a safer way to route the liquid by enclosing the drain. The supervisor determined that the risk was not high enough and put off the changes until a planned shutdown the following year. The company ultimately paid a $700 fine, that is not a typo, $700 dollars. Company officials argued that his proposed change was not related to the incident and would not have prevented it. I didn't know George; I only knew that this story scared me. As I mentioned earlier the Ultraformer, where we had a large fire in 2001, was a dangerous place. For those that worked on that unit, the next day after it happened, the next month, the next year, that stuff never leaves you and that leaves an impact. This story is a sad reminder of just how dangerous a refinery is. If you let your guard down for one second, that could be enough.

Chapter 4: Key Message(s)

Life is full of peril, short, and fleeting. Never assume tomorrow is guaranteed. Things will go wrong, be part of the solution. As I referenced on my introduction page, I have in fact seen fire and rain, probably even seen it rain fire.

In this chapter I learned courage and intrepidness

Chapter Five: The Big Shutdown

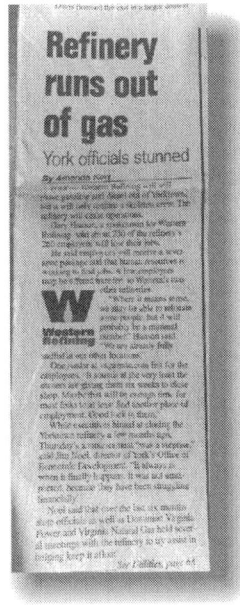

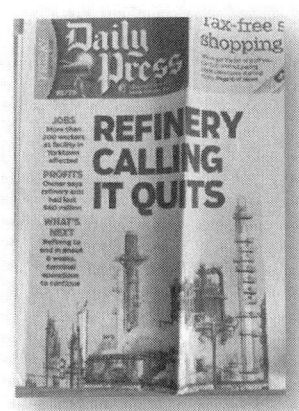

(6)   (7)

I don't remember the exact date, but we all knew it was coming. We were called to the pipe shop break room in the refinery, the entire workforce. We were told that the refinery was losing money, and they were pulling the plug. I saw grown men cry; it was stunning to hear. There were people walking out of the building sobbing. We were told when Amoco hired us, this is the last place you'll ever work, that always stuck with me. That was now over, at least for most in the room. My truck terminal move didn't seem so stupid anymore.

It was decided that the refinery would quit processing crude oil to make finished products, and instead would purchase those products on Colonial Pipeline, which was already connected to the refinery. Those products would come into our bulk tanks, neat or blended, and we would distribute them to the local markets. One of the places that product had to go, was through my truck terminal. I was in the right place, the customers and marketing folks knew me, I wasn't certain, but I knew my odds were good to hang around. After the big announcement, the company invited refiners in the U.S. and Canada to come in and recruit. Many of my colleagues moved to other parts of North America, a heavy concentration going to Fort McMurray, Canada, Indianapolis, and Houston. We were facing a reduction of three hundred plus, down to less than 30 people, 90%. My whole career I heard that you wanted to work on the process unit, that skill travels. They were right, it did. Fortunately, my skills stayed home. The move I made 5 years earlier would all but lock me in to stay.

Though I thought I was a lock because I was never interviewed for my position whereas many others were, I did have to go to the local community college like the rest of the remaining candidates to take a competency test. I never saw the results, but I presume I passed. Since we were moving to a terminalling business, I had the skillset needed to stick around. I was the only remaining person that knew how to run the truck terminal operations, the only. When the US EPA moved to ethanol in gasoline blending, I was hands on for the entire truck terminal rebuild. I knew the place inside and out, the business, the operation, the contacts. I knew I was making the right move in 2005 and in 2010 it paid off. I was one of the thirty.

Why the shutdown? There are many complicated factors, the primary ones as it was explained to me were as follows. Refining and marketing are extraordinarily complex businesses. The Gulf Coast refining complexes have direct access to major oil pipelines that run through the middle of the country. I don't keep up with it as much anymore, but at least at the time, oil that is delivered in the mid-continent region of the country, is bought and sold at a discount to waterborne crude oil. Sometimes that discount is as much as ten to fifteen dollars per barrel. The delta or difference between the cost of that feedstock, was enough to put the east coast refiners at a huge disadvantage. Since there are mountain ranges that separate both the east and west coasts from the mid-continent that make building a new pipeline difficult and cost prohibitive, the only easy way to the coasts is by rail. There are finished product pipelines that run from Texas all the way to New Jersey, those pipelines currently deliver nearly a third of the finished products that are consumed on the east coast, daily. The transportation infrastructure on the east coast is heavily dependent on these pipes for gasoline, diesel, and jet fuel. So, due to the economy of scale for the large refining complexes in Texas, combined with cheap pipeline transportation to the east coast, it is generally cheaper to pump a barrel of oil from Texas to Virginia, than it is to refine it in Virginia. That is good if you are a pipeline company, bad if you are an east coast refiner.

Photo credit- Daniel Cooper

Chapter 5: Key Message(s)

"Don't wait until you are thirsty to dig a well" Master Hsuan Hua.

Much like real estate, the key in refining is location, location, location.

Part III: It's a Terminal Now

The refinery had gone quiet, those sounds and smells were nearly gone. The address was the same, but this was soon to be a different world. The only active oil refinery in Virginia was nothing more than a scrapyard of millions of dollars' worth of piping, vessels, and other equipment. The hope was that some of the units would be sold, but most would end up being pieced out and the rest scrapped. I was in a new business, with new people, and soon to be in a new role.

Chapter Six: Same Address, Different Place

Since the refinery couldn't make a profit, Plains All American Pipeline came in to try a different approach. Over the course of a couple of years, we completely transformed the refinery into a terminal. What does that mean? We would utilize that same pipeline that essentially shut us down, to bring in products for blending and reselling. We would also construct new rail facilities and import crude oil to be loaded onto barges and moved back out to refineries. The facility that we built was capable of handling 208 railcars at a time. The purpose was to import crude oil from the fracking process that was relatively new, to bring American oil to the coast on rail, to be barged to east coast refineries. As fracking technology improved, the producers figured out a way to get it out of the ground at a lower cost. If that cost, combined with the freight rates on railcars to the east coast was low enough that there was a margin, the economics worked.

I ran the unit train and manifest train operations; it was a lot to keep up with. My boss Rich called me after the shutdown and advised me that I would be assuming the responsibility of moving the railcars in the plant. I was able to bring the person in from the contractor that had done it previously, he gave me one day of training. One day, to learn to move massive railcars of explosive propane, butane, and ethanol, talk about a crash course. I am rather good with running equipment, so it wasn't the end of the world, but it was a lot to learn.

Martinez- On the Other Side of the Fence

    I was responsible for training thirty people with no experience in fuel, on how to operate a massive crude unloading facility. It was chaotic, but fun. I was fortunate enough to recommend a few people who were eventually hired by the contractor, including my brother, cousin, and high school friend. We unloaded those 104-car trains, sometimes in as little as 6 hours. It was like watching a Nascar pit crew go to work in a well-choreographed dance. We were trained to operate the locomotives and had a few railcar movers called Shuttlewagons. I have moved thousands of railcars containing crude oil, propane, butane, and ethanol. That is one of the most stressful jobs I ever did. Those cars weigh 130 tons each. The crude trains were over a mile long. We had a looped track in our facility. If we had to circle the terminal to move the train from one track to the other, we would be moving east on one side of the facility and look across to see the back of the train moving west on the other side on the opposite side of the terminal. The power of the locomotives was incredible, the view from the cab is quite remarkable, and intimidating. On one occasion, I had to use our Shuttlewagon to help CSX rerail a derailed locomotive in our facility. The Shuttlewagon was a fraction of the size of the locomotive, it was terrifying to be hooked on to the back of that massive locomotive. We got them back on track, thankfully I only had to do that once.

    I learned the conductor role, the guy on the ground that connects and disconnects the train cars. The conductor is responsible for the consist, the train cars. What goes, what stays, where the car is placed in the order of the train. If the railroad brings you a train of thirty cars, the one in the middle may be the first one that has to be offloaded. Since you can't just pick a car up and move it, the cars must be cut and switched. For example, we might push ten cars to a side track, leave the middle car on the main, then go back and grab the others, now with the right car at the end of the consist. The job of shuffling the priority cars could take the entire day sometimes. It was slow, sometime just seemed like we went back and forth and back and forth.

The engineer, the person running the train, that was stressful. On the Shuttlewagon, due to its size, I couldn't see anything other than the black tank car in front of me, the end of the consist was a half a mile away, I had to rely completely on radio. A countdown of the distance starting at ten, down to one, then bang. I had to hit the car hard enough for it to couple. The car I hit had the brakes set, so it would move a few feet, then stop. At that point, we "stretched it out." We would pull the car back to ensure that the coupler locked. Once we had a good couple, we would call "all stop," then the conductor was safe to step in between the cars to connect the air hoses. Then and only then were they allowed to step between the train cars. Operating on and around trains is dangerous beyond imagination. The story the railroad trainers used to tell us was about someone getting caught between the couplers. They would say that if it happened to you, they would call your family before they pulled you out, because you would not survive it. I always appreciated the opportunity to work on the rail, it was a powerful addition to my skillset and really helped me understand every detail of that business.

Overall, the terminal world was relatively tame compared to the refinery. We had plenty of action and construction, but the risk of fire and explosion was much lower than the refinery, the element of high pressure and high heat, was mostly gone.

    As all these changes were happening and fifteen years from 1997, from praying for a job to feed my daughter, I was promoted to second in command. April 1st, 2012, the day after my son's ninth birthday and on April Fool's Day. I wasn't asked, there was no negotiating. It was a conversation like this, as of today, you are promoted to Assistant Terminal Manager, your pay will be X, and it is effective immediately. I'm not sure if anyone cared, or noticed, or if they thought I deserved it, to be honest. I like to believe that your work speaks for itself, and I hoped that I could gain the respect of people that were 20 years my senior when I started. I took a lot of time to reflect on how far I had come. It wasn't about deserving; I didn't deserve a lot of what happened to me early in my life. I felt as if I had put myself in the best spot and my hard work was recognized. I had gone from making $13.16 per hour at the bottom, to second in command. If hadn't gotten any higher in my career, I would have been at peace that I had made something of myself.

    I ran almost all the operations in the facility, trains, trucks, and everything in between. There was nothing going on in the facility that I hadn't done or supervised at some point, I always had the answer. I was also lucky, people liked me, at least the ones that made the decisions. One weekend, after severe storms, I took a ride out to check on things, as I often did. It was a big place, lightning strikes, or any number of issues could have surfaced following a storm, particularly with the big projects we had going on. As I was driving in, Jason Blevins who was a Vice President with the contractor building our rail facilities, was on his way out. We did the customary stop, rolled the windows down, exchanged pleasantries, and he asked me what I was doing there. I explained that I normally came out to check on things, I could see the intrigue in his eyes, we said goodbye and we both moved on. As fate would have it, a few weeks later, Jason joined our company as a director, becoming my bosses' boss. Sometimes things just line up for you, I could tell by that brief exchange with Jason, it changed the course of my life.

Following a good wakeup call at work with the refinery shutting down, I needed something to keep driving me forward and I found it. It was time to sharpen my mind. I graduated high school 407 out of 435 in my class, a 1.40 GPA. My objective was simply to do just enough to graduate. In my mind, I could figure out how those 28 people did less than I did. I wasn't into school, didn't want to be in school, and the only concern I had with school was how quickly I could get out of it. I graduated on time in 1994, after having to take a few extra classes to beat the deadline. School for me was the social network, where was the next party and who was I going to hang out with. All of that changed for me when I went to college in 2011, at the age of 35. I went to Saint Leo University which was located on the Fort Eustis Joint Army/ Air force Base, in Newport News, Virginia. When I took my entrance exam, writing was a breeze. Though it wasn't perfect, my time in the refinery helped me with that. My problem was math, I hated it. When I took my entrance exam, the algebra equations meant nothing to me. It was multiple choice, and I hoped I didn't accidentally guess one correctly, because it was a foreign language to me. I failed, for once I was relieved. I had to take a math prep class, and I was happy to. It was not easy for me, but I passed the class and aced the final with a score over 100%, answered all questions and the extra credit.

I was taking two accelerated classes at a time, four nights a week. It was a lot, but I absolutely loved it. I was the first to class, the first to turn in work, I turned in my finals usually before others had completed their mid-terms. I was so good at writing that I had to call my English professor one day because he accused me of plagiarism on a paper I wrote about the refinery. He wrote on the paper, "this is either an A or an F, how much of this is your own work?", I was furious. I called him and explained that I had spent my entire career in the refinery and that I was speaking from my own experience, passed with an A. I was only in school for a little over two years before being called away to manage a facility in another state, I never thought I could be so sad about not being in school.

A final highlight of note that I mentioned in the introduction, was speaking in front of the Virginia General Assembly. My boss Rich had confidence in me and since he couldn't go, he asked me to step in. Though I should have been, I wasn't nervous at all. We had recently started our crude rail business and there was an outdated statute on the books that our company was attempting to get changed and as far as I know, we were successful. Looking back at it, I would have to say that this is one of my career highlights, and something I never expected.

Chapter 6: Key Message(s)

I went from the class clown to the teacher's pet, I guess change is possible for anyone.

With trains as with life, sometimes they can be hard to keep on track.

Martinez- On the Other Side of the Fence

In this chapter I learned adaptability and embracing change with excitement.

Chapter Seven: Paulsboro, New Jersey

     I got the call, another life-changing moment and this was a big one. Though I wouldn't say I was confident in myself, I must have inspired confidence in others. Plains had a terminal in Paulsboro, New Jersey, a place I had never heard of before the call. I was at home, having just returned from a family vacation, still on the mend from back surgery, and the question came, would you mind helping at Paulsboro? Mind? I would love to. A chance to see a new place, learn new things, and did I ever. In New Jersey I learned about wooder ice, which the rest of us call icees, and a whole lot more.

     It was a mess, to say the least. There was missing inventory, harassment, theft, spills, asset integrity issues, low morale with a caustic work environment. It was bad. I arrived on a Monday morning at the Philadelphia International Airport and found my way to the terminal shortly thereafter. It would be hard to describe the feeling of tension and animosity in the air, but it was palpable. There was a sign on the front door of the business, the front door a multimillion-dollar petroleum facility, that read something to the effect of" Poor leadership, leads to poor morale, leads to poor performance". I had no idea what the assignment ahead of me was, but I started to get the idea quickly after reading that. I have never walked into a place where it seemed so many people were so angry, disconnected, and disgruntled. I was sent there and asked to help for a few weeks, before the day was over, I was informed I would be the temporary facility manager, that escalated quickly.

Fortunately, it was a blank slate, I had no history with anyone. I had to start paring things down and sorting them into compartments that I could work on independently. One being people, one being operations, one being customer service and repairing the damaged reputation. If you have ever managed a business, you will recognize that those are broad and complex issues. I had to get this turned around, while we continued to operate, without a spill, an injury, or a fire. There had been a small spill that was due to some very poor and risky decisions, that led to me getting the call to help in the first place.

Over the course of the next few months, I made a lot of changes. The customers at the facility had been used to the terminal accounting folks falsifying numbers, there was never an inventory gain or loss. In fuels, that isn't very likely, in fact it is almost impossible. The first month I was there as we sent out inventory statements, the first customer to respond had a 40 barrel, roughly 1700-gallon variance. Not a lot when you are talking hundreds of thousands of gallons of product, in fact that is about as good as it gets. The customer accused us of stealing their inventory, they weren't the last to complain. There was a fine line in getting this corrected, after all, the same company that brought me in was the one that was responsible for it happening. We navigated it and through relationship building, I gained their trust. I built many relationships in my abbreviated time there, with my customers, the town board members, and my employees, to name a few.

The struggle was real. There were many long and stress filled days. One of our customers had previously been allowed to operate their two leased tanks outside of safe limits. Mostly taking them below the established low levels. Essentially, the established safe limits of their two tanks were just shy of a full vessel load, so they had been allowed to pull them lower and established that precedent. Unfortunately, in doing so, we sustained damage to a pump due to the vibrations from the pump operating out of the pump curve. With excessive vibration comes the risk of seal failure and pump fire. When I explained to the customer that we couldn't continue to do that, they went directly to our commercial folks at corporate to complain. There were other tanks available for the customer to lease, but that would have cost money, so they wanted to keep pushing the limits instead. Despite the pressure, I drew the line and said I am not going to be responsible for the terminal burning down over something we all know isn't safe, and the practice stopped.

There were other occasions, my operations manager almost decapitated himself driving the terminal golf cart early in the morning, right through a cable meant to keep vehicles out of the tank dikes. Luckily for him, the cart had a roof, and the cable mangled the metal poles holding the roof, and not him. On another occasion, a driver that had been barred from the facility for a multitude of safety violations, returned to the facility looking for a way back in. He was a large, grumpy, and muscular tough guy. When he came back to beg for forgiveness, he was a little different, to put it lightly. He came in on a Friday while I was on my drive back to Virginia. I got the call from my two main guys, informing me that this guy came in begging. As he walked in the office, he got down on his knees and offered oral sex to them if he would be allowed back in. The guys told me that they turned it down, I wasn't there to know one way or the other, so I had to take them at their word.

Before I left, one of our customers from Freepoint Commodities called me, she said "I hate to hear that you are leaving, no matter what was happening, I always knew when I called that you would take care of it". She said, "Just the sound of your voice on the phone and your accent would put me at ease". She meant that in a very professional way, but it was reaffirming that my customers were put at ease by talking to me, and that I had a country accent and sounded like a bale of hay.

I was also invited to a dinner with many airline fuel executives, whom I provided fuel for at Philadelphia International Airport. I was told by the General Manager of the Fuel Facility at the airport that this was the first time a terminal person had been invited to the dinner. I was accompanied by my two main guys who helped me with the turnaround of the facility. Once the meal got started, there was a speech where I was asked to stand and be recognized for turning around the facility after some big struggles. I was toasted and there was a round of applause for me and my team. It was humbling, I was a long way from the truck terminal in Yorktown now. This dinner and what I did there led directly to my future success. Plains was selling the terminals in the region, Paulsboro and Philadelphia were finished product terminals and not really part of Plains core business. After a few months there, I was advised that we would sell the terminals and asked to stay until that happened. I found out later that I was in the contract to purchase the terminals, that I would stay on for a period after the sale closed, again very humbling for me. The buyer approached me soon after the sale was announced, and offered me the same position with them, as the Terminal Manager. I had dinner with one of their Vice Presidents one evening. He said to me," there aren't many times in your life where someone is going to come to you and ask, what is it going to take? We need you there and we are willing to pay you to stay with us". I had never been in this position before and it was quite a lot to digest. They offered me almost $40,000 a year more than I made at the time, almost a 40% raise.

While this was going on, my boss in Yorktown advised me that he would be leaving for an opportunity and that his role would be opening as well. He knew that if I wanted it, it would be mine. I had a decision to make before most people even knew about either position, it was a tough one. I had been in Paulsboro for almost a year, building a team and building relationships. I had grown significantly in that year, especially in my confidence, thanks to my commercial manager and eventual friend, Kory Clement. On the worst days, when it seemed the world was falling apart around me, I would call, and she would always help me work out whatever problem had come up. I had been on my own and it was a resounding success. The market had not been great around that time and one of our commercial people told me at one point that my facility was the only one in the company that outperformed the planned guidance. The reason, they didn't plan for any. The facility had not made money and under my direction, things turned around.

I guess the thing I learned about leadership and integrity that made it so tough, is that you can't tell people you are building something, and then walk out. Don't get me wrong, people do, but that isn't me. You might hear someone say, the company doesn't care about you, you're just a number, but that isn't why you do it. You do it for the people that helped you get there. While companies might buy and sell facilities as they fit the model or don't, in many cases the people that work there don't leave. They count on you, if you don't take that seriously, you shouldn't be in leadership. Not long after, my boss in Yorktown made his announcement and I got the call. We want you to run Yorktown, WOW. It was surreal, even though it was somewhat expected. I had to decide and as hard as it was to leave what we were building; it had been a rough year on the road, and I was ready to stay home for a bit of a break. It wasn't final, but I had at least decided what and where my preference was, Yorktown.

Around this time, I was still helping in Paulsboro some and Yorktown some. When I got the call to run Yorktown, the offer was too low. For the first time in my life, I said no. After a rough year in New Jersey, I knew the stress I was taking on and I was not going to do it for free. The Division Director, Mr. Robert Mcleod, whom I admired and respected, called me. Robert and I figured out the number I needed, and he made it happen. It was less than I was going to make in New Jersey, and the facility was three times the size in Yorktown, but I was home and that was hard to put a price on. Leaving Paulsboro was incredibly sentimental, it had been my breakthrough. This was my place, my team, my people. The crew and the new company that took over, threw a surprise party for me before I left. There were around twenty-six people who showed up, VP's, directors, terminal folks, their families, and they had it at my favorite pub. They brought me gifts, they shared stories, and more than a few shed tears, yes tears. In less than a year, the people that had no idea who I was or what I was about, were in tears that I was leaving. I hope that everyone can experience that in life at least once, feel how it feels to have a positive impact on someone else's life, and have them affirm that with tears. That was another one of those moments I will never forget.

Chapter 7: Key Message(s)

One day you have been somewhere for 18 years, the next day you're in New Jersey. I guess you just never know what tomorrow holds.

In this chapter I learned what true leadership and humility are.

Chapter Eight: A Different Siege of Yorktown

I am not sure if I can convey in words what my first day as manager of the Yorktown Terminal felt like. I bet the only person that was prouder to claim Yorktown than me was George Washington himself in 1781. My office was now the refinery manager's former office where for most of my career, if you were lucky enough, you could be on that floor in the building, maybe peek in. If you screwed up, you might be unlucky enough to see it, but that wasn't how you wanted to see it for sure. There were people now reporting to me, who had been there since I was born. The same people that taught me everything I knew, now worked for me. Not in my wildest dreams in 1997 when I prayed for a job on that fishing pier, would I have believed this one. I am certain that the jury was out on me, I am certain there were people who didn't think I deserved it, it didn't matter, I would prove them wrong.

My first struggle, this is how we have always done it. I am a firm believer in looking at all options. How do you know the best way, if you only know one way? I didn't mind shaking things up, and I did just that. I changed the mechanical contractor that had been in place since I started working there, I changed roles, responsibilities, and attitudes. One of my first days on the job, I went through the security gate and a guard asked, "can I shake your hand"? Of course, I said and proceeded to shake his hand. I laughed and said, why did you ask that way? His response, "the last manager never took the time." That resonated with me, and that short interaction taught me something that I hadn't really thought of before. I was now in a position of influence, where my actions mean something to others. People are watching what I do, different people for varied reasons. Some people watch because they want you to fail, and they wait for it. Others watch because you are their leader, they respect the position and hopefully respect you, eventually. They want to learn from you, they want to know what made you successful, so they can be. You are under a microscope. I wanted people to respect me for the job I did, not the position I had.

    This was a large facility with a lot going on. The operations part came easy for me, that was second nature. We differed from many terminals in that we were very self-sufficient. We had our own spill response team, rail car movers, emergency response team, we did it all. With all of that came a lot of regulations and many inspections. In my time as manager, we had a large spill response drill that was covered by the local newspaper. There were more than two hundred people involved in this drill from a multitude of agencies. There was a fire department drone, video room to monitor the river and area of response, and a corporate incident command center set up in Houston. I presided over all of it, a lot of pressure but an amazing opportunity to gain valuable experience. I would only spend about two and a half years in charge, but I believe that I earned the respect of my former co-workers and peers, with many of them still reaching out to me to this day. It was a rewarding experience and having come full circle in 20 years, from bottom to the top, was something I will always treasure and in many ways, it is still hard to believe.

As a good leader, I am always thinking about the next move, preparing the facility for the future. I was also a bit lucky. One of the people that I always looked up to as a young operator was Sean McNulty, who shared some stories in this book. Sean had gone to work for Suncor in Fort McMurray, Canada, following the refinery shutdown. After a few years, he decided to return home and was working at a car dealer at the time I reached out. Sean was also a high-ranking officer in the refinery fire department, as well as another local department. I knew there was a potential that I could leave at some point, which eventually materialized. I brought Sean back as my operations supervisor, and that paid dividends not long after. It is crazy how life works, from someone that mentored me, to reporting to me. I was probably happier about Sean coming back than he was. I knew what I was getting, a proven commodity. A funny story about Sean when he came back to work for me, he hates this story. One day I asked him a question about something, he didn't have the answer. He had only been back a few weeks, I said, "no big deal". The next day, he comes to my office prior to our morning meeting and says something to the effect of, "sorry I didn't have the answer but here is the answer." I said, "don't worry about it, you haven't been back long, no big deal." Sean looked at me and said, "yeah but you know how it is when your boss asks you a question that you can't answer, you feel bad." I looked at Sean and said, "no, I don't know, that's never happened to me." I laughed; he didn't think it was as funny, I guess. Sean was a great man to leave my team with, I am grateful that it worked out that way.

Around September of 2018, I received a call from my former customer at the airport in Philadelphia. It was common for him to touch base occasionally, but this one was a little different. He said, we have a position in Orlando, and it is a bit of a mess. What you did in New Jersey needs to be done in Orlando. My response, I appreciate the thought, but I am good where I am, and I don't want to waste anyone's time. His response was, "worth a try." A few days later, he calls back and says" my boss wants you to waste his time anyway." It happened that I was going to Houston in a few weeks anyway, so the meeting was set.

    As we met and I was interviewed, I was also conducting an interview of my own. Randy Davies was the Senior VP of all fuel facilities in our company, covering most major airports in the United States and Canada. Randy was my kind of guy, a great guy and down to business. I wasn't nervous, I didn't really have anything to lose. I had been working in the same facility at 2201 Goodwin Neck Road since 1997 and it was now 2018. I started at the age of twenty-one and now at the age of forty-two, I spent half of my life there to this point. I had been in every role, at every level. I had been offered positions at other places, but this was the one. For the second time in a few years, someone asked me, "what is it going to take to get you"? And this time I gave an answer. I weighed in and lobbied for Sean to replace me, and he did. The plan worked perfectly. I was off and I left my team well cared for with Sean. It was time to fly.

Chapter 8: Key Message(s)

"We started at the bottom now we're here" Drake.

"Luck Is What Happens When Preparation Meets Opportunity" Roman philosopher Seneca

Martinez- On the Other Side of the Fence

In this chapter I learned self-appreciation for my journey and efforts.

Chapter Nine: A Camper, an Airport, and a Dream

So, the part I left out, I left a place that I had been for 21 years, to work for a contractor on an expiring contract, eight hundred miles from anyone I know. I bought a travel trailer to live in, and in 8 weeks I would make a long drive to a new place. I had a lot of time to think about the decision on the drive. I wasn't sure if I was stupid, crazy, or just confident that I was the person for the job. In hindsight, maybe some of each. I entered an entirely new world, without connections and the network of people that helped make me successful in my prior facilities. I was in the airline industry, highly compensated, and had the weight of the world on me, but it was exciting, invigorating, and new.

I drove my truck connected to my camper trailer to St. Cloud, Florida, the day after Christmas in 2018. I had everything I would need for the next six months contained within. That 800-mile drive was the first time I ever towed a camper, when I got to Florida, I swore it would be the last. With every pothole, I thought I would certainly meet my demise, particularly in South Carolina. Once I got to Florida and got set up, I was ready to go to work. The situation worked well for me. I had no cable or internet, other than my phone. I was there alone, and the lack of distraction allowed me to jump in with both feet. I could work weekends or whatever I needed to do. I was isolated, but it was right for the situation. When the afternoon storms came through, that was a different story. There were a few storms that I thought I might be blown to a different campground.

Instead of trying to find an apartment or a hotel, it was really the ideal thing for me to do and I am glad I did. After my six-month term was up, I found a house and was able to deal with all the other stuff, but at least I had a good handle on work.

The aviation fuel business is unique, and like most petroleum, a small world and circle of people. I had the great fortune of working for some fine people in the airlines, particularly Tom McCartin of Spirit Airlines, formerly of Southwest Airlines, and Joseph Burrows of Southwest Airlines, along with Randy Davies of Menzies Aviation. When I needed buy in before, it was from my boss and my crew, this was a whole different world. I worked for a contract operator, who operated the Fuel Facility at Orlando International Airport. Technically I operated the Orlando Fuel Facilities LLC, which is a business formed by the member airlines at the airport. I work for the Fuel Consortium, in addition to the contractor, in addition to the Greater Orlando Aviation Authority. Confused? So was I. Basically, I have a lot of bosses.

I would like to take some time to explain some things about how an airport works, at least as much as I can share. Much like the refinery, an airport is a city within a city. There are subjects that I cannot touch on for security reasons, but just some insight on the day to day. Most major airports have what is called a fuel consortium, which is responsible for the operation of the common use fuel facilities. Many people don't think about fuel when they are in the airport wondering where their plane is, or if it will be on time. There is so much behind the scenes. A

74

complicated network of fuel piping, trucks, pumps, tanks, and I am only speaking to the fuel side of things. There are bags, trams, tugs, lavatory trucks, everything must work on every single flight. A fuel consortium exists so that the multitude of airlines that might fly to a particular airport, don't have to go build their own fuel tanks. This enables airlines to have flexibility, to fly to markets that work and not to ones that don't. They can scale up or scale down proportionately.

Aviation fuel is highly regulated, as it should be. In this business, a plane cannot pull off the road if there is an issue. We go to great lengths to ensure fuel quality, from the beginning of the supply chain all the way to the fuel cart or truck that you see hooked to the wing. It is a highly audited business; it is nothing for us to have thirty audits in a year. These audits are conducted by airlines, environmental enforcement agencies, the fire department, and the list goes on.

When we have too much or too little fuel, there is a system in place that allows us to put out alerts from the fuel operator to the airlines, these alerts go out worldwide. Those alerts can request an airline to bring enough fuel so that they take none from an airport, take as little as possible, or even the other direction to request for them to take more. That is a tricky process. Jet fuel weighs nearly 7 lbs. per gallon. For a plane to take extra fuel, causes it to burn more fuel. Some smaller planes on certain routes cannot tanker fuel one way or the other, the same with bigger planes that are travelling long distances.

In my six years at Orlando International Airport, not including 2024, there have been over 220 million people that have flown through the airport, with an estimated 60 million more in 2024. In essence, my team and I are responsible for the lives of every single one of them. One fuel quality issue could be catastrophic; therefore, we have a zero-fail mission. I am responsible for millions of dollars' worth of fuel that is issued every day, in addition to multimillion dollar operations and maintenance budgets. My job is no small job.

    As I mentioned before and back to the beginning of my airport experience, the operational part was easy. I had to learn the airline and airport world; I had to learn where the hell I was half of the time. I was focused on the job, the rebuild, the problems, but still in awe of how far I had come. I was responsible for the fuel operation at one of the busiest airports in the world. How did this happen I would think? How did I navigate all this strife to land here? However I got there, I did it. You might think that isn't a big deal, it's not like I am famous, or anyone knows me. To me, I have now arrived at a place that is so far above anywhere I thought I would ever be. I did it. When Randy hired me, I heard from him and several other people, Orlando used to be the model. Orlando was where they would show off to our customers, how we did things. I said it as plain as I could, my expectation was that it would be again. I have control now, control of our expiring contract, our performance. Everything was on the table, if I failed, I didn't have a security blanket. My livelihood and that of the thirty or so employees that worked for me depended on the decisions I made and the actions that I took. I was on my third crew, my third facility, and my third state for that matter, in 4 years. Though each place had its own challenges, they all had them.

The situation wasn't good, but I had seen it before, and I was brought in to repair it. We had many good folks, and some that wouldn't be around long. Randy had been around aviation for countless years but recently came to the contractor that I worked for, prior to hiring me and I didn't want to let Randy down. Though I can't detail the issues, I came to find that I had some good people, who had been done a disservice by someone that was absent in the operation and in any leadership capacity. In my first meeting at the airport, just a few weeks in, things didn't go so well. The airport was kicking off a large terminal expansion which is now in service and known as Terminal C, and in this meeting in particular, the focus was the fuel system. Apparently, one of the engineers that represented us on the fuel consortium side, had made quite a bad impression. He had been poking one of the construction VP's a little too often and I believe that he came to the meeting for one purpose, to set our engineer straight. As I sat with him and shortly after the meeting started, the VP said a few words, then he addressed our engineer directly. He said, "I don't want to hear anything from you, no calls, no emails, nothing." He then looked at me and said, "that goes for you too." That was my welcome to MCO. Our reputation wasn't good, and it showed quickly, we were starting from zero.

We had some folks that had been empowered by the lack of leadership, not in a good way in some cases, forced to make decisions because there was no one else that would. The ones that tried didn't get support. We had to make a few changes, some hourly and some salary. Once I established a culture of accountability and order, things started improving. Professionalism, how we conduct ourselves, becoming a part of the airport community, letting people know who we were and that we wanted to turn the ship around. Aside from the internal changes and credibility with the airlines, we began by establishing a relationship with the airport fire department, also known as ARFF. I had a lengthy history in emergency response, and this came easy to me, we spoke the same language. The fire department conducts audits quarterly based on the FAR 139 program, that is regulated by the Federal Aviation Administration. Though we didn't have any glaring issues, there were minor ones that should have been easily corrected. During the second audit where we had the same simple issue, enough was enough. I warned, the next time this happened, whoever was responsible wouldn't be here for the third time, it never happened again. We had a multitude of other issues, the employees told me that they had reported them multiple times with no results. There were several similar instances of this, they were all resolved very quickly.

Within the first year, I was invited to train the entire fire department on our fuel operation and response tactics. Roughly 75 professional firefighters, all focused on what I had to say. Some of the people in attendance had never been to the fuel facility or had only driven through. Bear in mind, aside from a plane crash, the fuel farm is worst case scenario at an airport. Potential for catastrophic damage, injuries, loss of life, impact to neighborhoods, the environment, and last but certainly not least, operational disruption to one of the largest airports in the world. I began with my background, showing a few illustrations of some of the events I had personally responded to, credibility. There were many questions, lots of good feedback. Of course, we provided lunch, and everyone knows that is the key to a firefighter's heart. This training became annual and when there were special events, such as our new tank construction, it became more frequent. During the construction of the tanks, I developed a presentation that I projected on the inside wall of one of the new tanks. The purpose, to show the responder how the tank is built, why it's built that way, and how the tank behaves in a fire. This time, we not only had the ARFF group but also the City of Orlando firefighters in attendance. In all, there were well over one hundred people, and this was not the only event that we would hold for this group. Some of the local Orlando firefighters told me that they had been with the department for over 20 years, driven past the facility countless times, yet had never stepped foot in it or understood exactly how things worked. This is how you build relationships, it's how you become part of something.

This example of relationship building extended across many airport departments, another example, social media. In 2021, we executed a big project to clean and recoat our bulk storage tanks. To continue relationship building, I requested and received approval from my boss and the airport, to place a large decal on the tank that faces the public, with the hashtag #flyMCO, which I believe may have been the first ever on a tank. This is the social media handle for the airport, what better way to connect than to put the social media handle on a tank. I posted a picture of it, not long after I received a message from the highly acclaimed social media team, "is that really on the tank"? Absolutely. They asked if they could come over and take some pictures, maybe do a story on us, absolutely. They did just that a few months later, posted a video of me narrating the fuel farm tour to be seen by their many thousands of followers. That wasn't the reason I did it, but very cool just the same. I became close with that entire group, anytime we held an event, everyone wanted to be there. It brought people together, built connections, relationships, happening without you even thinking about it.

As my bosses did before me at the terminal, we held quarterly and bi-annual contractor and safety appreciation luncheons. These turned in to quite the spectacle, with sponsors clamoring about who could do the next one. Tricycle races, dunking booths, food trucks, you name it, we did it. We had a seafood boil that had well over 130 people in attendance. People flying in from other states, clear across the country. That is what team building looks like. Fire department, airlines, city or airport officials. I am in the people business; I must be an expert at it. I could write twenty pages of examples of successes at Orlando between my team and me. One of the main construction managers and a friend were telling someone else one day, while I was standing there, that when we were in the room with the airport Chief of Operations, it was almost embarrassing how much he praised us. One act at a time, we established that we were now a part of the solution instead of being a part of the problem. We have a brand, a reputation, and we guard it carefully.

In 2020, I had the unfortunate distinction of leading my team through the Covid-19 pandemic, one of the worst times in the history of commercial aviation. We went from distributing more than a million gallons of fuel per day to less than one hundred thousand. It was a crazy time, there were mass layoffs in aviation and lockdowns everywhere. We were essential employees; in the early days we went to work not really knowing what was going to happen. On one hand, we didn't want to buy in to the hype and on the other we saw the news, people were dying. After having gone through all of the years of worrying about a shut down that came to realization, now I am leading people through the worst pandemic in 100 years. We wore our masks, we did what we had to do to keep the airport running, and we went home. At one point during the Delta variant, my team and I would complete our day jobs around 5 p.m. and then go to assist with loading bags onto airplanes, when there weren't enough people to do it. We came in on weekends, worked late, whatever needed to be done. Not one of us got paid a dime to do it, and not one complained. I was grateful that we had our jobs, and we would do whatever needed to be done to keep the airport running. There were a limited number of people that could do what we were doing, due to the special credentials that were needed to be around international flights. Customs agents would come by and check, to be sure that we had them.

    We held our meetings outside; we had letters to present that we were essential personnel should we get pulled over for being out during the lockdown. We had protocols to follow, and we did. If we had an outbreak, it could have seriously jeopardized the operation of the airport. The only good thing to come from the pandemic was that there wasn't much traffic. Unfortunately, a lot of that traffic that was missing were our customers. During that time, Florida set up a checkpoint on interstate 95 as you entered the state, I believe they restricted entry to those coming from New York and New Jersey. Florida was otherwise open for business and more or less became the Covid hotspot. We didn't lose anyone in my group but there were a couple of people that worked with us through our fueling partners that passed away from Covid. I had seen a lot in my time as a refinery worker and facility manager, but I never had pandemic on my bingo card.

Outstanding Leadership Awards

We were coming out of the pandemic, though things slowed down, Florida never stopped, and it ramped up quickly on the back end of the pandemic. On January 19th, 2021, I was invited to join a call with Southwest Airlines, many of my peers were also on this call. It was not uncommon for us to do this for procedural or organizational updates with the airline, but this was different. I thought nothing of it when my boss told me to be sure I was on it, I just assumed that meant it was mandatory and that everyone got the same message.

As I sat listening, first they announced that there was an award given to our company in Atlanta, for outstanding service provider. I don't remember the details but there was a great improvement in the into-plane fueling business that they provided. Into-plane fueling is the process of connecting a fuel cart or truck from the hydrant system in the ground, to the plane, and fueling it. Our company leadership was pleased that we had won the award, our competitors were also in attendance and this award covered all stations that Southwest Airlines operated in.

The second award was up, and the speech began. One of the managers from Southwest, the one that I worked for, began to talk. He described a lot of things that had been done, that sounded like things I had done. He described broken morale, broken infrastructure, and all the things that needed to be repaired. He then went on to say how things had improved, how amazing the turnaround had been, and how every airline that flew into MCO would benefit from our work. Then he said it, the 2020 Southwest Airlines Outstanding Leadership Award winner, Graham Martinez,

MCO. I was stunned. Sam, my assistant manager, was sitting next to me when it was announced. He was patting me on my shoulders, smiling, shaking my hand. My phone started ringing with text messages, phone calls, it was like winning the heavyweight championship of the world, to me anyway. To this day, I cannot describe the feeling, the gratitude. There is no amount of money, there is no bonus, there is nothing that could replace the feeling of this award to me. From where I started, to here, this was an improbable journey. I will be forever grateful for that award, it hangs, framed behind my desk. Since my early 20's working in the refinery, I set the highest bar for myself. With this award, I reached a place that just wasn't supposed to be for me. It doesn't matter to me what anyone else thinks about the award, it is about the journey that I took to get here. The adoption, bankruptcy, cheating, the stress, the fires, everything, it all culminated here to me. To this day, this is my greatest professional accomplishment, more on a second award in a minute.

In addition to the Southwest Airlines award, I was also nominated for the National Petroleum Management Association for General Manager of the Year 2023. Though I didn't win, I was honored to be in the conversation, and I will work even harder now. More than money, the ultimate compliment in business is to be recognized by your peers, particularly the ones that are exposed to the entire network that you associate with.

It isn't all about me, nor should it be because this is a team sport. In 2022, category five hurricane Ian struck the Fort Meyers area of Florida. The storm devastated that area, and then Orlando, with flooding that had not been seen in modern times. There was approximately fifteen inches of rain at the airport in less than 24 hours. My Assistant Manager Andrew, our hurricane crew, and I would ride this event out for three days, without leaving work. Our team had to keep water pumping out of tank dike walls, to prevent damage to any equipment or a tank from floating away. Subsequently, we had to remove the water that had accumulated in our hundreds of hydrant pits where the airplane fuelers connect their equipment, to return the airport to service very quickly. During that event one of our mechanics drove into a flooded road and had to be rescued by the airport fire department. The next day, after all hands-on deck, we were back up and running on time. For that effort, Andrew went on to win a global award for teamwork. Globally our company has more than 35,000 employees, Andrew won the award. My accounting manager, Chris Self, was also nominated for the global award for customer service, having worked through a fuel crisis that could have shut down Orlando International Airport. That is what a winning team looks like.

      On September 12, 2024, I was awarded my second Outstanding Leadership Award at the Southwest Airlines Fuel Summit in Dallas, Texas. I would like to say I deserve it or expect it, but neither was the case. I work hard, I am dedicated, but there are many others that are. When you are competing with every other station that Southwest Airlines operates at, it is even more humbling to win a second award. I honestly felt guilty about winning an individual award, I have 30 employees that keep the fuel flowing at Orlando International Airport. The first morning safety meeting after I returned to Orlando, I thanked my team. I dedicated the award to my team. I do not deserve an individual award when my team does the work, so that award is for all of them. When the award was announced, it

Martinez- On the Other Side of the Fence

was all I could do not to tear up. My boss Randy was there, and many of my peers. Walking up to shake hands and receive the award in front of so many of them felt like slow motion and a blur at the same time. I wonder now, as I did when I won the first one, do other people appreciate this like I do? With that award, I won two of the last three Outstanding Leadership Awards, 2020 and 2024. A fueling manager from another company won it in 2021, I know him and it was well deserved. Southwest did not have the awards in 2022 and 2023 for assorted reasons, hence the two out of three. I have always been told the awards have to be "spread around", to win a second one was a distinct honor and something I will never forget.

Southwest Airlines Outstanding Leadership Awards

85

Our team has been recognized repeatedly for various awards and accolades. We have been asked to mentor other locations, audit them, assist them, support them in hiring, you name it and we do it. My goal at the beginning of this was to make Orlando the best again, I think we are close enough to say mission accomplished.

Chapter 9: Key Message(s)

Teamwork makes the dream work. Don't ever let anyone else decide how high you can fly, your destination belongs to you and the effort you put into it.

In this chapter I learned the value of persistence. It's not how you start; it's how you finish.

Part IV: Leadership Mentality

I live for leadership. Leadership is not a burden; it is an honor. Leadership is not a task; it is a gift. Whatever position in management you are in, someone believed in you. They promoted you, in most cases because of the technical skills that you had. Some of you may have been promoted, because you were the best option, you were the best of the undesired. Whatever the case is or was, if you are reading this, you probably care about becoming a better leader. As a leader, especially one in a dangerous business, there is one call that you never want to make. That call is the one to a family member, saying there will be an empty seat at the dinner table. Your father, mother, sister, brother, boyfriend or girlfriend won't be coming home. This is a real possibility in my business, one that enough people don't consider. One that is waiting there for us every single day. What I have learned about leadership is trust. When you are faced with life and death, you need trust. Trust in each other. At that moment, all else fades away. You have your team, and you have the situation. You can sink or you can swim, it is a matter of life and death. What I do as an airport general manager, is also life and death. Your family or mine could be on that plane.

Doing the right thing when no one is looking, means all the stuff in the background, before that fuel is in a plane carrying your family. It means not taking shortcuts, unnecessary risks, or chances that don't need to be taken. As a leader, your people watch what you do, just like children watch their parents. If you take a shortcut, even when you think no one is looking, that becomes a habit.

You set the tone, on your worst day, your best day, and all the days in between.

Celebrate Your Wins, Learn from Your Losses, like a football coach in the locker room after winning a game, dancing and singing and sipping champagne. We like to win, we want to win, and we work hard to win. There is validation in winning, overcoming adversity, and prospering. What about losing? Losing makes us better. If we lose and we don't learn, then we truly lose. If we lose and we learn, then we don't make the mistake again. That is how we sharpen our skills, that is how we get better. Some losses are more painful than others, those are the ones we learn from the most. In the airlines and my previous company, we had a process called a safety management system. In my previous company, it was known as Plan, Do, Check, Act. What does that mean? Any job you do, any task, you plan it. You lay out how it is supposed to look. You do it, execute the job. After the job, you compare the plan vs. the execution, you figure out what worked and what needed to be improved, so you checked it. Then you act, you act to implement the changes to make it better the next time. That is how we learn from our failures, we must acknowledge them, face them. There is another saying, you can't fix what you can't face. If you can't accept your own failures and realize that you have them, you can never improve.

The one thing I think that stands above all is servitude, the desire to help people. There is a saying that people don't care what you know unless they know that you care, I believe that. The more you think you know and the less you think others know, the less likely you are to get others to follow you. People need to see the vision, to believe in the mission, and to want to execute it. If they know that you care and you paint the big picture for them, only then can we work towards the finish line of that common goal. At the end of the day, we are compensated to perform tasks. In our case, our basic mission is to provide clean fuel to the sixty million people that fly through Orlando International Airport annually. That is the mission but it's not the goal. The goal is to be the absolute best at everything associated with our operation, bar none. If there was an award for the best airport janitorial service, we would have the cleanest facilities in the land.

Chapter Ten: Old Fashioned Hard Work

As I said above, we all love to win, that part is easy. Staying humble in victory is important. When you are successful in life, usually you have put the work in. There are many people who will judge you and be jealous of your day in the sun, but those people weren't there in the trenches. They didn't see the work you put in, and they want the attention, earned or not. Let your work speak for itself. You don't need to tell everyone what you have done, assuming you work for good leaders, they will recognize you. What if I don't work for a good leader, usually that has a way of working itself out as well. Bad leaders in many cases do not run a high performing team, and bad results generally lead to a change in leadership. Moral of the story, own both your successes and your failures equally. I keep the leadership award that I won hanging behind my desk, I see it every morning I walk into my office. On the other side of my desk is a sign that was given to me by my team, it has my name and under it says" Great Boss = Great Team". Recognize that if you receive something like that, there isn't a higher compliment, pure gold. Your team will decide how much effort they give you, usually it is based on how much you give them. They can decide to do just enough not to get fired, or they can go above and beyond. As simple as a concept as this seems, I have in the past and continue to witness managers that do not understand this concept. There is no outstanding leadership, without outstanding people to lead. Period.

Once I understood how leadership was supposed to look, I equated it to winning, and I wanted to win, everything. I wasn't a quitter, never again. As I mentioned earlier, I had breathing problems from an early age. As I started in the refinery, I was lazy. I don't know if I knew it at the time, it was just who I was. One of my best friends Don Wolfe, who worked for a vendor in the refinery, convinced me to start running one day. Don is probably the smartest person I have ever known and if he isn't, he is on the shortlist. Don and I hung out all the time and one day we went for a run, I probably made it a quarter of a mile. He didn't beat me up, he pushed me. I think at that point, I was ashamed of myself. I remembered those words my dad said to me years earlier, "once a quitter, always a quitter". I didn't want this to be me. I would continue to run, faster, farther, and I would make the gym a part of my daily routine. Don gave me the kick I needed, I never looked back, he changed my life with a little push. Once I got the taste, I became a gym rat. I found a way to lift or run nearly seven days a week.

When I was no longer on shiftwork and went to day shift, it became very easy. I was addicted to it, don't get me wrong, no addictions are good, but this one was a high I couldn't get enough of. I studied, I read magazines, internet articles, you name it, I was up on the latest. I could tell you the protein count in a can of peas, or anything else you wanted to know. I aspired to be a certified personal trainer; I was just never able to quite put it together. What I found in the gym was my outlet, the release and the escape. I could literally exercise the demons. It is crazy how people start noticing and talking about you when you get in shape. I would hear the comparisons, or one of my favorites was who would win in a fight in the refinery between me and another guy who was in good shape also. When I was at my peak, I benched 315 and I was running 5k runs in 20 minutes and 37 seconds. I felt like I was on top of the world. I had rules in the gym, if I saw someone lifting 5-days a week, I lifted 5-days a week, or six. If I was on a treadmill running and you got on one next to me, I wouldn't stop until you did. If you ran 6.5 miles per hour, I ran 7.0 miles per hour.

As a member of the fire department, we had to get an echo cardio stress test every couple of years. I asked what the best time was when I got to the doctor's office to do mine. I knew that no one could beat me, but I wanted to make sure it wasn't close. The way the test works is that you begin by walking, and they gradually increase the speed and the incline. I explained to the nurse at the facility that I would be trying to make sure I went longer than anyone else, by a significant margin. She laughed at me and explained it wasn't a competition, but to me it was. I heard that 14 minutes was the time to beat, I was barely breaking a sweat by then. The further I went, the faster and steeper it was. By the time I got to 20 minutes, I had enough, and figured no one would get close. I was basically sprinting uphill at that point. Once I climbed off the treadmill, the nurse rushed me over to connect the EKG leads. She called over to the doctor and said, "we've got a live one", while laughing. I later confirmed, no one else got above 14 minutes. To me, everything was a competition.

Around that time in the refinery, we had a fire on a resid tank in the refinery, a heavy black oil like asphalt. There were flames coming from the vent on the tank. As soon as I heard about it, I rushed as quickly as I could to get my bunker gear on. Once I got to the scene, Chief

Dickie Burroughs said, "I need someone to go up and get eyes on this", this was my job. I answered before he could finish asking, and off I went. Everyone that knew me knew that if it needed to be done and I was there, I was doing it. I wanted to be first at everything, I ran to get to the top of that tank. It wasn't a terrible fire and besides that, I was invincible in my bunker gear.

I was a big Ultimate Fighting Championship fan, and I had the determination and drive to train to fight, so I decided I would see what I could do about it. I was around 32 years old, and though I took karate as a kid, I didn't have any other experience other than fights in high school. I searched and found a place that trained fighters, East Wind Academy of Martial Arts, in Newport News, Virginia. I was in heaven. At that time, I worked out or ran 7-days a week and added training for MMA 4 to 5 days to that. I even attended a seminar with Dan Inosanto, who was opposite Bruce Lee in the nun-chuck fight in the movie "Game of Death". I started out learning some basics in Muy Thai and other martial arts, I wanted to get to a cage fight, but again, I felt I wasn't good enough. In this case, I wasn't. My dream of a cage fight would not materialize, one torn calf muscle and nagging back pain that would lead to surgery would end that dream, probably for the best anyway, I couldn't afford to lose the brain cells.

What does all of that have to do with leadership?

I don't accept failure, excuses, or being a victim to anything. I will determine my fate. I determine how hard I run, lift, work, lead, or anything else I do. These stories in the gym or in a meeting room, I have the same mentality, a fear of failure. I hate losing. In my experience managing people, it is as simple as working harder than the next person. Most people are not willing to do what needs to be done, without entitlement, without complaining, without the feeling that they are owed something that they haven't earned. Success is simple, it is simple for me, and it is simple for anyone that works for me. The world is easy today, it is easy to shine. It is rare that people are willing to put the work in and if you are, you win, most of the time. The other part is patience, it doesn't happen when you want it to most of the time, it happens when it happens. In my case, God's timing or my lucky stars, whichever way you see it, has worked out for me every single time. I am not implying that I am the toughest person on the planet, far from it. I have an office job, and I want to be the best that has ever done that job.

Another thing about being a leader is being someone that people want to help. Building a network of people to lean on, and who lean back on you when they need it. I have built that network, comprised of former coworkers, contractors, consultants, peers, you name it. I don't know it all, there are always things that come up, the trick is having someone to answer the things you can't, the same way you answer things for them. I want to see people succeed, and I want to help them do it. I am in a position of influence, and I want to take advantage of that in the most positive way I can, to help people that have helped me.

I have trained and mentored more people than I can count. It is truly a blessing. One thing that I try to do is put myself in their shoes. I try to explain things from the perspective of the person listening. I have identified some great talent, from various walks of life and levels of experience. I do not hire people based on what they know, I hire them based on who they are. My job is not rocket science, it is a matter of repetition. I find that with the right person, I can take them as far as they want to go. With the wrong person, I'll get nowhere. You just can't teach someone who is convinced that they already know everything.

I believe in extreme teambuilding, every member of my team is as important as the next, the lowest person on the totem pole is as important as I am at the top of it. Why? Because one mistake by them can have catastrophic consequences, how good of a leader can I be if my team is failing? I force my managers to complete two performance evaluations per year, including a review with each employee, where that employee gets a chance to provide feedback and thoughts. An employee should never hear about poor performance for the first time, in one of these meetings. I force my managers to have these conversations, good or bad, twice a year. If it is an uncomfortable conversation, the manager isn't doing their job. Gentle nudges along the way throughout the year, keep people on course. Waiting to do that twice a year, or even worse, once a year, is not good leadership. Why wait until it all comes to a breaking point?

I have been asked to go to many places that were failing, assess why, and report back. Almost without fail, when I go into an operation, one of the first things I hear is a manager say that I want to get rid of him or her, this guy or that guy. I do not believe that people are generally inclined to do a bad job when they are properly motivated, compensated, and appreciated. When I hear that "I want to get rid of someone", that tells me immediately that there is a management problem. It costs money to replace and train people, new people expose the operation due to a lack of familiarity. In my former human resources training, there was a message that said, "hire right, manage easy". There is so much truth in that. New people are a blank slate, that's good and bad. Management must evaluate their competency and spend an enormous number of resources training them. Is the devil you know better than the devil you don't? Sometimes. If you have taken the time to hire, train, and get someone out in the field doing a job, shouldn't you try to keep them? If you as a manager are even thinking "I want to get rid of this person", you aren't doing your job. The other common phrase is H.R. won't let me, nonsense. It isn't about H.R. or the employee, it is about you. If you ask yourself a couple of questions, this is an easy problem to fix. Have you given the employee clear expectations and are you following policy. It is really that simple. If the employee is truly not salvageable, following policy and procedure will allow you to walk them right out of the door. More importantly, if the employee is not meeting your expectation, you need to ask yourself if you have given them that clear expectation. How is someone supposed to meet the goal if they don't know what it is? Like running a race but not knowing where to go or for how long.

Furthermore, does the employee know the big picture, do they know the mission. When I was in those big fires, I knew the mission. My leadership gave me a specific task, to do my part, to accomplish the bigger mission of putting out the fire. Aside from the tactical aspect, people want to know what they are fighting for, what they are working for. People need to know the mission. At the airport, our mission is to provide clean fuel, in whatever quantity is needed, to the American public that wants to visit Orlando. The job we do, day in and day out, is all dedicated to that end. My team is important to me, even the weakest member. I don't care how good you think you are, in our business or any leadership, you cannot do it alone.

It is about setting a standard and keeping it. Holding every employee to it, every single day and every task. I will not look the other way; I will not let your attitude hold my team hostage. If you aren't part of my team, then it is time for you to join someone else's. In the words of the coach of the Pittsburgh Steelers and fellow Denbigh High School alumni, "the standard is the standard."

A practical example of real-world leadership that I can offer would be during the large fires that I responded to. There were a few times when I was asked to put myself in very dangerous situations, in the middle of those fires, closer than most people would dare go. I trusted my fire chief. I felt that Chief Burroughs would not send me into a situation that I shouldn't be in. I was confident in his training, his decision making, and my ability to do the job, in other words I trusted him with my life. I emphasis again, I trusted him with my life. Some qualities in a leader are taught, some they are born with. Like any dangerous profession, police, fire, or military, a good leader can inspire you to follow them to the gates of hell. Chief Burroughs passed away recently, his leadership is something that lives on in me and I hope that I can inspire others, the way that he did me.

One thing I mentioned there is related to integrity in leadership, my integrity has been tested many times in my position and I will share a quick story about one occasion. When I worked for Plains All American Pipeline, in 2018 they rolled out an award called the "Goal Zero". The program was meant to foster a healthy competition amongst the facilities in the company. To obtain the "Goal Zero" trophy, my terminal had to go through the entire year with zero accidents, zero injuries, and zero controllable spills. In 2017, we had gone through the entire year without any of those things happening. In late 2017 during our annual budget meeting, I had several projects that in my view were necessary projects. My terminal was not generating a lot of profit, if any, so it was never fun to go through the process. As I was leaving following our first day of meetings, my boss pulled me aside and told me "If you don't cut some of these projects, I will." My response to him was, every project that I have in the budget is either regulatory compliance related, or facility integrity, and there were none I could cut.

    The next morning when I came in, my boss made cuts as he saw fit, against my will and better judgement. One of those projects was for one-hundred thousand dollars, for a continuation of removal of abandoned refinery piping that was left to rot and full of product or residue. He made the decision and that project, among others, was wiped away. Unfortunately, about 6 months later, the inevitable happened and someone who was out doing routine patrols saw a large spill that had spread in the pipe alley for about two blocks. The pipe alley had been full of water, so the oil on top looked much worse than it was but ultimately, we determined the spill to be around 18 gallons. I had all hands on deck for the cleanup, there were more than 15 people there in addition to our environmental coordinator.

    Once we had the scene secured, I called to notify my boss. I advised him that we had an approximately 18-gallon spill. I explained to him that it was abandoned piping that leaked, but I never mentioned the fact that he cut it from the budget. It wasn't appropriate in my view in my attempt to be professional and respect his position, but deep down I wanted to say that this was your fault. One of my first thoughts, we just lost our Goal Zero award. My boss asked me when I told him the size of the spill, "are you sure you have a spill?" If I said no, our record would remain unblemished, and I would get my award. But I didn't say no, I said "yes, I am sure". I said that for a few reasons. The first, because it was true. As a leader, how would it look for me to stand up at the end of the year and accept a hollow trophy that I know I didn't earn. What would that say about my integrity to the 50 people that reported to me and every single one of them that was out there covered in mud with me cleaning it up? Two, I wanted to prove the point that the project should have been done and if you keep deferring maintenance, this is what happens. The bottom line, I don't want to win a trophy if I had to cheat to get it. Despite the regulatory reporting, and the endless calls to answer for it, I would not compromise my integrity. I think that I gained the respect of my team for that. As a facility manager, there are a multitude of government regulated plans I must comply with. In the back of those plans is an attestation, my name goes on the dotted line. Something that loosely says, I will comply with all requirements of this plan, non-compliance can result in fines and imprisonment.

It is easier for someone in a corporate office to defer maintenance, provided they aren't the one that signed that plan. Aside from that, what does that say to your boss that you are willing to lie? When you go through an interview, you are asked about your integrity and why it is important, for me that doesn't stop at the interview. I never got one of those Goal Zero awards, but I did pick up the hardware from Southwest Airlines, so it all worked out in the end.

There is also bad leadership, unfortunately I think it is the standard and not the exception. Following are a few examples of that. It may be a bit quirky, but I have a personal sticking point about calling someone boss. If I refer to you as boss, that means I respect you. It may be a simple delineation but that is where I draw the line.

When I was working in the refinery, only five years in, my supervisor asked me to train one of the other guys in the control room, then another. These were guys with roughly twenty years of seniority on me at the time. I had no issue training anyone, I was all for it most of the time. My only stipulation was that the person had to want to be trained and be engaged, in other words not distract me and waste both my time and theirs. The first one had little to no interest in the job, he was more interested in looking at the stock market and whatever else was out there. I don't think he made it very far and he was back in the field soon after that.

The next runner up was a guy that I liked very much. Sometimes he was engaged and sometimes not. One evening he took a few hours of vacation prior to coming in to participate in his bowling league. When he got there, I filled him in with the details of the current operations, and it was busy. Within the hour, he was asleep with his head on the console next to where I was trying to work. He didn't participate for most of the rest of the night, my biggest aggravation was having to work around him to do my job. The supervisor walked by a few times and saw him sleeping, doing nothing about it. I got busier and busier, at one point walking into the supervisor's office to find him asleep as well.

    I bit my tongue, choosing to keep the peace, until about five in the morning, an hour before shift change. The supervisor came in and proceeded to tell me that I should have asked him about some decision I had to make in the absence of anyone else being conscious. I apologized and explained that I walked in, and he was asleep, so I didn't think it was my place to wake him up. As I listened to him, I finally had enough and calmly said, I don't feel comfortable training people in the control room anymore. I was one of the newest and youngest control room operators in the refinery, that was my excuse. To me the job was easy, but I needed some reason to free up the keyboard of the guy sleeping on it, without getting my coworkers in trouble. He then got mad at me and to quote his words "you just don't want to work with anyone, do you?"

    Before all of this happened, I had made my position clear that I didn't want to be on his shift. He was a poor leader, one that would take credit for your work and blame you for his shortcomings. He was also one who assigned me all of the jobs that the lazy people didn't want, because he knew I would do it and do it right. There were times when the shift guys were playing cards, he would see them playing cards and have me do their work. I had about all that I could take after all of this. I would intentionally time my work to miss shift briefings by climbing my tanks for inspections during lunch, or whatever it took. I was miserable and I was tired of being taken advantage of.

    So, after the morning conversation and all the things that had been boiling over for a while, I walked into the supervisor's office and said that when I got off in a few minutes, I was going to be waiting for the superintendent to come in that morning. I told him that I was going to explain how I was being portrayed to be the bad guy, while people slept, played cards, and how he was one of them. I turned and went back to the control room. He walked back in and told me, "I will let you off of the shift." While I was relieved, I didn't want to be known as the problem and creating waves. It was a difficult spot because the bottom line was, I just wanted to do my job. I could give a few more examples, but I think you get the point.

    This example is the very opposite of good leadership. Taking credit for others' work, making good people do the work of the lazy people, not following policies, not leading by example. The crème de la crème of the poor leadership awards in my view is rewarding laziness and punishing the best worker. I can honestly say that this is one of the few times in my life that I absolutely dreaded going to work. My goal then, as it is now, is to never allow that work environment to exist under my leadership. I will say this in writing, the day that it does, is the day that I recognize that I don't belong in leadership.

Chapter 10: Key Message(s)

Life can be fun when you make a competition of it, it can also be a giant pain in the ass. Make your leadership as much of a competition as running a race. Constantly improving your time and position, never settle for where you are, there is always more race to run.

Poor leadership ruins good people. There are some good leaders out there, learn from them, ask questions.

Recognize the bad qualities of a bad leader, learn from them, and never, ever, repeat.

A good leader can inspire you to run through a wall of fire in a way that makes you look forward to the trip.

In this chapter I learned patience, the hard way at times.

Chapter Eleven: We Won't Quit

What is worse than having cancer? The answer is easy for me, my only son having it. Just maybe those refinery days have come to haunt me. In August of 2023, my son was diagnosed with Thyroid cancer. Hearing those words was like an out of body experience. I fell apart. Why him? Why does my son have to go through this? He is a good kid, never been in trouble, never any drugs. Why? Sometimes that is just the hand you are dealt. I couldn't sleep and I couldn't accept it. I cried like a baby. The shock of hearing that and having to tell my son that was the hardest thing I have ever done, bar none. I would have walked through 100 refinery explosions, not to have to do that. I never read the handbook on how to handle this. I have had family members that have battled cancer, some won and some lost. This is devastating. My son is the kind of kid that everyone loves, he never had a bad report card. He makes people laugh, he will always lend a hand or play a prank. He played sports in high school, he likes doing what other young men do at 21, video games, play golf, basketball, mess with his car. I just kept saying to myself, he doesn't deserve this. It was a horrible nightmare.

When I sat there with the surgeon for the first time, when she said they would take his thyroids, I felt like I would collapse. Once the initial shock had worn off, I heard this saying, over and over, if you are going to have cancer, this is the one you want. I heard it is 100% curable. We got through the first surgery, the radioactive iodine treatment, tough times. You never want to see someone you love having to go through this, but it was what we had to do. This diagnosis changed him, and it changed me. Given all that I had gone through, I had to figure out a way to get through this. We have many things to be thankful for, the fact that we caught this and got started early is certainly a blessing. Second, living in Florida, we are amongst the best cancer centers in the world.

Another thing I am thankful for, the prayers. For most of my life, anyone that has known me has known my son. The well wishes, the prayers, it all matters. Sometimes a few simple words in a prayer can make the difference in your day. I am thankful for friends like Jason and Kara Hobbs, they spent the entire day at the hospital with us during his surgery. In this day and time, everyone is busy. If you have someone that supports you like that, stay close to them. This situation hasn't left my mind since the first word of it, but I am learning to process it and try to keep things in perspective. There is a saying to the effect of, 99% of the things you worry about, never happen.

At some point, you realize that there is a lot in this world that you don't have control of, this is one of those things. The feeling of helplessness while your child is in an operating room is one of those things. What I learned through this was a lesson in humility, of what it is like for the people that count on me. The people that work in my operation put their faith in me. They count on me to keep them safe and to put bread on their table. I had to put my trust in the experts, I had to hope that they took their job as seriously as I did. In their job, lives depend on them, well it is the same in mine. Once we were referred to the Moffitt Cancer Center, I had to let go of my fear and put my faith in God and in the science. I had to keep my head up, I had to believe, truly believe in the positive outcome. That is the only way to get through a dark time like this.

What you believe or don't, is for you to decide. For me, the power of prayer leads to the power of positive thought. That positive thought leads to a positive outlook, and that positive outlook is what gets me through the day. We all need something to believe in, something bigger. I grew up going to church, I said prayers, but they were just prayers. This is targeted for a specific outcome for a specific person. I saw the light, and I have seen the power of prayer. I have seen how it has affected my ability to function, to get me through without worrying, I am thankful for it.

Life ebbs and flows, peaks and valleys. In my life, I have known what it is to fight. Life will test you and you have two options, push forward or give up. I am hardened, galvanized, but not jaded. I appreciate the struggle, because it taught me how to appreciate the good times. I appreciate the struggle because it taught me humility, compassion, and perspective. I wouldn't be the leader I am without it. This fight is doing the same for my son. Life owes us nothing. When all else is stripped away in this world, our jobs, titles, awards, our health is all that counts. Everyone has a fight. As a manager or leader of people, it is most important to understand that everyone's life isn't like yours. In many cases as a manager, you live a better lifestyle, have material things, don't have the strain of paycheck to paycheck. That fight is one that many people have, and some will fight it for their entire lives. I was one of those people. I was as poor as I could be, resigned to the fact that my life was one of struggle and poverty, some of my own choosing. If I take this situation back and apply it to my mentality then, I certainly could not have dealt with this adversity then as I would now. I am thankful for my struggles, more now than ever. On this topic, I will apply the same mindset as any other I mentioned above. We must win, because failure isn't an option. I will trust in God's timing, because that has never failed me.

Chapter 11: Key Message(s)

"Let me tell you something you already know. The world ain't all sunshine and rainbows. It's a very mean and nasty place and I don't care how tough you are, it will beat you to your knees and keep you there permanently if you let it. You, me, or nobody is gonna hit as hard as life. But it ain't about how hard ya hit. It's about how hard you can get hit and keep moving forward. How much you can take and keep moving forward. That's how winning is done!"
Sylvester Stallone, Rocky Balboa

In this chapter I learned to have faith in God, there are some things that are beyond my control.

Epilogue/Conclusion

So here we are, you have read my story from the lowest low to the highest of highs. Through the struggles and crazy trials and tribulations, I have learned to appreciate the art of leadership. I took all the bad things, I took all the good things, and I used those to figure out who I am. I am passionate, if I put my mind on or my heart into something, I cannot be stopped. I have been beaten down and I have been helped backed up.

A refinery life is an amazing and complex life, it takes a small city of people to operate it. some incredibly intelligent people, hardworking people. You learn things about fuel that you never even questioned; you learn things about life that you didn't expect. Like a family, some people are closer than others, but when it was time to come together, you put all of that aside. It was an amazing privilege in my life, to be a part of that. To experience the camaraderie that some could only imagine. To work in a refinery is to know how the world moves. You learn to take the good days when they come and think about those to get you through the bad ones. You learn what it is to see a friend hurt, what true stress is when you are waiting in your bunker gear at the firehouse to see if that problem is going to subside, or if your training is going to be put to the test. You learn to trust people with your life and the value of life, yours and theirs.

The refinery was the building block of my legacy. Leaving a legacy means everything, why? Because I wasn't supposed to have one. I wasn't supposed to be anything, and I was well on my way to that. On this journey, the discipline that we have determines our path. The effort, the relentless effort, the refusal to quit. Sometimes what seems like a harsh word, such as "once a quitter, always a quitter", will stick with you. It will drive you and be the fuel that you need when you think you want to quit. If you know nothing else know this, I won't quit. An integral part of being a leader is fortitude. Not quitting, not tapping out, not taking the easy path. You cannot lead people if you are seeking the easy way. Double down on the things you don't know and that you don't like to do, do it until you think nothing of it. That is how winning is done. Like a fight, you cannot run and win, you must face the fight. When the fire siren went off, I ran to it, not from it. Do the thing that you don't want to do, the hard thing.

On leadership, be the leader that you want leading you. Treat people and speak to them the way that you want them to treat and speak to you. Respect goes a long way. Never forget that no matter where you are on the journey, we all want the same thing, to feed our families and have the best life possible. Recognize your people, the same as you want to be recognized. Never fake it, genuinely care about the people that depend on you. Their lives are literally in your hands. Seek opportunities to learn leadership, if you think you know it all, you're not a good leader. A good leader is always looking for a way to be better, period. Most of all, take pride in building other leaders. You will put in your years as a manager and in the grand scheme of things, that will be a short time. Your legacy will be in the people that you develop and help along the way. Your impact can spread far and wide, it can grow exponentially. If you train five leaders and they go on to manage their own business, with each of them training five, your leadership impact continues to expand. You can change the world, one employee at a time. In a world where everyone is trying to fit in, trying to fit the mold, create your own style. Never do just enough, leave your mark, make your legacy.

    Hopefully, you will take one thing from this that will make you a better leader. The people that help you in your life are like the rungs on your ladder, each one giving you the opportunity to climb one step higher. Thank those people frequently, as much as you may want to think you did it on your own, the chances are, someone helped you. Your job as a leader is to become that rung for the next person. To sit in the back of the room the way my boss did, and smile when your person wins that award.

    One of my great friends Kevin Holifield likes the saying, iron sharpens iron. Surround yourself with good people, work hard, be a good person, in other words, put yourself in the best position to succeed. From nobody to managing people and money beyond my imagination, to ensuring the safety of airline travelers from around the world, what a journey it has been.

    Love what you do and do it with a smile, it goes a long way. I wish you all the same success that I have had and countless blessings.

Bibliography

This book contains stories based on firsthand accounts of the author. All opinions and descriptions of these events are told from their perspectives and do not necessarily represent those of the company, or any other persons associated with these events.

(1) Lee, P. (1990, April 15) Are Refineries Unsafe?: Petroleum: A recent series of fatal fires and explosions at oil and petrochemical plants has raised questions about the industry's safety practices and use of contract workers. https://www.latimes.com/archives/la-xpm-1990-04-15-fi-1951-story.html

(2) Hydrogen Sulfide information-
https://www.osha.gov/hydrogen-sulfide/standards

(3) Hurricane Rita - Source National Weather Service
https://www.weather.gov/lch/rita_main

(4) Paust, Matthew. "Yorktown Refinery hit by fire." Daily Press (Newport News, Virginia) November 2005

(5) O'Brien Root, Kim. "Fire Doused at York Refinery". Daily Press (Newport News, Virginia) September 2006

(7) Cawley, Jon. "Refinery Calling It Quits". Daily Press (Newport News, Virginia) August 6, 2010

(6) Kerr, Amanda. "Refinery runs out of gas". The Virginia Gazette (Williamsburg, Virginia) August 7, 2010

Acknowledgments

To Matthew, my best friend, never stop fighting.

Mom and Dad, you chose me. You didn't have the money or the room, but you did and you made it work. I owe you both my life.

Kyle O'Leary, thanks for the random post about leadership and choosing me as the focus of it. That post, in no small part, inspired this book.

To my brothers, thank you for allowing me to be one of you. I could never know your perspective on things, but hopefully now you know mine.

To Jason Blevins and Robert McLeod, thanks for believing in me. You made decisions that changed the course of my life.

To Eric Kelly, thanks for teaching me the art of leadership. I am not sure if you truly understand the impact you have on people like me, but it is life changing.

To Randy Davies, Tom McCartin, thanks for taking a chance. Two of the best bosses I could ever ask for. You gave me the space to create my vision, to allow my humor into my work, and hopefully to change the game.

To Kory, thanks for making me believe I was good at the three things. When times were rough, you were always there to help.

To Joe Burrows, thanks for affirming what I aspire to be, an outstanding leader. I will treasure that award, but more so the kind words that came with it, for the rest of my life.

To Joseph Storey, thank you for the second award. I guess the first wasn't a fluke after all.

To Kevin Holifield. Your enthusiasm for your workers is genuine and infectious. Your struggle wasn't very different from mine. Thanks for showing me how leadership is done and for being my friend.

To all my current and former employees, thanks for buying in. I could never be a great leader, without having great people to lead.

To everyone else that helped me in my journey from nobody to somebody.

About the Author

Luis Graham Martinez has been in the petroleum industry for 28 years. With experience and expertise in emergency management, multi-modal fuel movements, and most recently a key figure in jet fuel movements in the central Florida region.

- Father of two

- General Manager Fuel Facilities Orlando International Airport 2019- Current

- Southwest Airlines Outstanding Leadership award Winner 2020

- Southwest Airlines Outstanding Leadership award Winner 2024

- Mid-stream petroleum terminal management expert

- Refinery operations and management

- Runner Up Southwest Airlines Silver Nozzle Award 2021

- Nominated for National Petroleum Management Association for General Manager of the Year 2023

- Business Logistics Saint Leo University 2011-2012

- Keynote speaker Yorktown Virginia Rotary Club 2016

- Panel member SAIM Connect Conference 2023

- Emergency responder in multiple major refinery explosions with specialized training from Delaware State Fire School and Williams Fire and Hazard

- Former member national strike team Plains All American Pipeline

- Guest speaker at Virginia General Assembly in reference to HB 845 (2014)

Made in the USA
Columbia, SC
25 February 2025

54399396R00076